CONTENTS

FOREWORD

When Tennessee celebrated its Bicentennial not long ago, one fact became clear: our state owes its progress and promise to its people. Some of their stories are captured here.

T. Jensen Lacey offers an entertaining collection of facts, oddities of history, and tales both true and tall.

—Governor Don Sundquist

PREFACE

If there's ever a way to make people fall in love with a state, it's to ask them to write a book about it. Since I took on this project, not only have I found more reasons to love Tennessee, but I've discovered more about Tennessee than I ever dreamed possible. Having worked some years back at the Museum of Appalachia in Norris (and now living in Middle Tennessee), I seem to be the perpetual tourist, curiosity seeker, and history buff. There's always a curiosity around the next corner, or in the next town. Go down any highway in the state and there will be a historical marker that tells just enough about something to make you want to know more. And beyond that marker, there's always a "Believe It or Not" kind of tale. The inspiration behind this book has been those intriguing stories, anecdotes, and bits of history that make Tennessee a state of endless fascination.

I've tried to include a little of everything in this book, so you never know what the next turn of a page will bring. You, too, are on a mission to discover more, laugh a bit, and be amazed, touched, or inspired as you read along.

There are always more curiosities to be written about and more tales yet to be told, so if you think of something that should be included in future editions, please write me in care of my wonderful publisher.

For those of you who don't live here, maybe this book will entice you to visit. Join me now in my love affair with Tennessee, and enjoy.

ACKNOWLEDGMENTS

I'd like to offer special thanks to Governor Don Sundquist for writing the foreword; my father-in-law, Richard C. Lacey Sr., for his help in the legal department (thanks again for bailing me out); and my parents, Marian and Joseph Jensen, for proofreading.

I thank the people of the chambers of commerce throughout the state for their assistance. Many others assisted me, as well. Cherry Condra Ralston of *Tennessee Backroads Heritage* and the staff of the Tennessee Historical Society gave help and advice. Ron Lotz of Lotz House Civil War Museum advised me on Civil War facts. Patrick Glynn of Wireless Flash News Service searched ten years' worth of their quirky news items on things related to Tennessee. Ed Hooper, historian and broadcast journalist (who maintains the site Tennessee Online), stayed available day and night to answer my sometimes obscure questions. Barbara Parker and Elizabeth Phillips, of the Tennessee Department of Tourist Development, disseminated my requests to people throughout the state and reviewed the text. Donna Rea of the *Erwin Record* set me straight on how Mary the elephant was hanged. Mike DuBose, Muriel Anderson, Amon Evans, and Dave Steighan offered me their invaluable tales. Don Wick, Tennessee historical trivia buff, helped me fill in the gaps. Ralph Emery, celebrity interviewer and himself a celebrity, looked over my chapter on "The Sound of Tennessee." Actress Patricia Neal reviewed my text and offered me friendly encouragement. Ashley LaRoche, assistant editor of *The Official Tennessee Vacation Guidebook* and the magazine *Tennessee Connections,* both published by Journal Communications, provided never-ending assistance. Old buddies Carlock Stooksbury and John Rice Irwin of the Museum of Appalachia shared East Tennessee lore, photos, and the drawing of the still (I'll never tell where yours are located). Marie Tedesco, archivist at East Tennessee State University, researched photos. Stephen Cox, curator at the Tennessee State Museum, provided many photos. Kassie Hassler of the Tennessee State Library and Archives did research and provided information. Authors Vernon Summerlin, James Crutchfield, Phila Hach, and Richard Cornelius gave assistance and advice. Dr. William Foster, professor of historical linguistics at my alma mater, the University of North Alabama, Florence, provided information on speech and linguistic patterns unique to Tennessee. Sportswriter Larry Schmidt looked over the sports section. The librarians at Nashville's Ben West Library, Austin Peay State University's Tennessee Room, and Clarksville Library (especially Tim Pulley and other reference room librarians) provided much assistance. Ron Rogers, computer whiz, gave me technical advice for the inevitable computer troubles. Ludd Trozpek of the Lewis and Clark Trail Heritage Foundation and Byrne Dunn, publisher of the *Lewis County Herald*, provided help on facts about Meriwether Lewis's grave site. Dr. Sutton Flynt, dean of the College of Education at Austin Peay State University, and his wife, Deb, proofread the manuscript and did not cover their ears when I told them Tennessee anecdotes. The staff of the Tennessee Film Commission supplied facts on the movie-making industry here. I offer Jerry Ray and Mike Gabriel a special thanks for the James Earl Ray story and pictures. I thank Ted Crozier for being my courier; I owe you an errand or two. I am grateful to a thousand other people who were friendly, helpful voices over the telephone lines. I also want to thank Larry Stone, my publisher at Rutledge Hill Press, for his visionary attitude toward this book and for his faith in me, and Jennifer Greenstein, my wonderful editor.

And finally, I wish to thank my immediate family for putting up with me while I wrote this book.

1
Truly Bizarre Events and Notorious Tennesseans

"I Got This Six-Point with My Chevy Pickup": The Road Kill Bill

TP# 2

In 1999 Representative Tommy Head (D-Clarksville) and Senator Tim Burchett (R-Knoxville) sponsored the "Road Kill Bill" in the state house and senate. The bill proposed to make legal the keeping and consuming of wild game, such as deer and bear, killed by motorists. The house passed it, 95-0; in the senate, there was only one dissenting vote, and Governor Don Sundquist allowed it to pass without his signature.

This legislation was the topic of many comedy talk shows, such as *The Tonight Show with Jay Leno,* but the politicians themselves were not without a sense of humor. For example, when asked his opinion of the legislation, Senator Steve Cohen was quoted in the *Tennessean* as saying, "This is really a Jewish Mother's bill. 'There are people in Europe who are starving. Eat it.'"

The Road Kill Bill gives a whole new meaning to the term "Bumper Crop."

A Weird Gastrointestinal "Bug"

In the summer of 1869, when a girl in Murfreesboro named Thankful Taylor was chopping cotton, she stopped to drink from a nearby spring to cool off. From then on, she began having stomach complaints. At first doctors thought she had a tapeworm and treated her for it, but it didn't help.

Finally, five years later in 1874, she again sought medical help, since her stomach was getting no better. The doctor found the complaint, all right. He reached into Thankful's mouth and pulled out a twenty-three-inch-long brown snake! The papers don't say whether she checked her drinking water source after that.

Not Quite Ready for *The X Files*

In Lebanon, Tennessee, in 1997, an antique-store owner named Frank Buster reported he was in possession of a severed space-alien's head. He had bought it from someone who said he'd run over the "alien" in his pickup truck and buried the rest of the creature's body. Buster had taken the head to a taxidermist for stuffing and mounting.

After some of the local press came to check it out, it seemed that Buster had been made the butt of a joke. The mounted object looked more like the shaved backside of a deer!

Notorious Tennesseans

Tennessee has more than its share of colorful, notorious folks. Here are just a few.

★ **The Harpe Brothers:** Micajah ("Big Harpe") and Wiley ("Little Harpe") were bloodthirsty thieves and their story is a grim one. They started out stealing stock from their neighbors in Beaver Creek around 1797, but they went on to robbing travelers, often murdering them in the most gruesome ways. For example, one man named Johnson was robbed, killed, then cut open, filled with stones, and tossed in the Holston River.

Big Harpe made his fatal mistake in 1799 when he killed the wife and baby of a man named Moses Stegall. Stegall rounded up a posse and caught Big Harpe in Kentucky. Enraged with grief, Stegall reportedly decapitated Big Harpe with a butcher knife—while he was still conscious. His head was hung on a stake at a crossroads (called after that Harpe's Head) in Highland Lick, Kentucky.

Little Harpe didn't learn a lesson from this, for he continued to rob travelers along the Natchez Trace. He was caught and hanged at Gallow's Field in 1804, near the trace.

★ **John Andrews Murrell:** This amoral outlaw with the air of gentility was launched into crime at an early age by his mother, a hotel owner near Columbia, who taught John and his siblings how to rob from their guests. He grew up to become a horse thief, robber, slave stealer, and murderer. The most infamous of his acts, though, was a regional slave rebellion he tried to arrange in 1835 whereby on a set day the slaves were to turn on their owners and kill them. It wasn't that he was sympathetic to the plight of slavery; he hoped the resulting chaos would make his looting easier. The plot was discovered and more than fifty white men and an unknown number of black men were banished, hanged, or beaten. Murrell was tried and convicted of this despicable act and sentenced to nine years of hard labor in the Tennessee State Penitentiary in Nashville. He died in 1844 in Pikeville, shortly after his release from prison.

★ **William Walker:** Born in Nashville in 1824, Walker was a brilliant man, academically. He was one of the youngest graduates from the University of Nashville in 1838, and then he earned his MD degree at the University of Pennsylvania in 1843. He also studied in Edinburgh, Scotland, and became a lawyer.

Then he decided he wanted to rule a country. In 1853 he went to California, formed a small army, and attempted to conquer Lower California and Sonora in Mexico. This failed and the U.S. government arrested him for violating neutrality laws. Soon freed, he invaded Nicaragua and became its President in 1856–57. Then he was forced to leave. He tried to gain control of Honduras, but he was captured and executed. History calls him "The Grey-Eyed Man of Destiny."

★ **Edward Zane Carroll Judson ("Ned Buntline"):** Using the nom de plume Ned Buntline, Judson edited and published in numerous Nashville publications, including the *South-Western Literary Journal.* Accused of having an illicit relationship with Mary Porterfield, he killed her husband, William, in "an altercation" on March 11, 1844. When William's family came to lynch Judson, he jumped from the City Hotel's third floor to escape them, and ultimately left Nashville.

This man became known as "the King of the Dime Novelists" and also launched the show business career of Buffalo Bill Cody.

★ **"Colonel" James Russell Davis:** Born in 1840, this colorful character is said to have been a member of a Confederate guerrilla group that operated independently during the Civil War. Davis once tried to enter a cross-country car race but couldn't renew his driver's license because he was 108 years old. Davis claimed to be Cole Younger, a member of the James Gang, and he appeared with J. Frank Dalton, who claimed to be the real Jesse James, on the TV show *We the People* in 1950. He died two months after this appearance.

★ **Annie Cook:** After the Civil War, this attractive woman of German descent opened a brothel in Memphis, called Mansion House, one of eighteen in the city. When the yellow fever epidemic hit in 1873, she dismissed her "working girls" and turned Mansion House into a hospital. In 1878, when the fever gripped the city again, she repeated this charitable act and earned praise from Christian ladies' organizations. Unfortunately, Cook herself became a victim of the disease and when she died, the *Memphis Commercial Appeal* gave her this editorial eulogy: "Out of sin, the woman, in all the tenderness and fullness of her womanhood, merged, transfigured and purified, to become the healer." Cook's work inspired some of her "girls" to take up nursing as their new profession.

★ **George Maledon:** It's always good when people like the line of work they're in, but George Maledon was especially devoted to his. He was an executioner, who personally hanged sixty of the eighty-eight men sentenced to death by Judge Isaac Parker, the famous "hanging judge" of Fort Smith, Arkansas. At times he sprang the trap of as many as six people at once!

Along with his twenty-one years (1875–96) of professional executing, he is credited with killing five would-be prison escapees.

After Maledon retired, he was a colorful storyteller in the Federal Soldiers' Home in Johnson City. He took pride in doing his job right the first time, for he liked to say, "I never hanged a man who came back to have the job done over." He died in 1911 and is buried in Johnson City.

★ **Kid Curry and Annie Rogers:** Harvey Logan, known to history as Kid Curry, and Delia Moore, really Annie Rogers, were members of the Wild Bunch. Their leaders were Butch Cassidy and the Sundance Kid. Kid Curry was captured in 1901 after a shoot-out with Knoxville police. Annie got into trouble when she tried to exchange five hundred dollars in stolen Montana bank notes at the Fourth National Bank in Nashville that same year, but Curry helped get her acquitted, saying he gave her the money. He then escaped from the Knoxville jail in 1903, tried to join Cassidy and Sundance in South America, but failed. He fled to Colorado, where he finally shot himself and saved the legal system the trouble of executing him for his misdeeds. Annie's fate remains a mystery.

★ **Night Riders:** For several months in 1908, masked riders wreaked their own form of justice on people affiliated with the West Tennessee Land Company. The Night Riders, composed of men and women who lived in the area, had always taken much of their subsistence from Reelfoot Lake, but the land company had secretly bought it and planned to drain at least part of it and turn it into cotton fields. Most of the public sympathized with the Night Riders, seeing the terrorism as a form of self-defense. On the night of October 19, 1908, some of the Night Riders kidnapped two of the company's officers, Quinton Rankin and R. Z. Taylor, from Ward's Hotel in Walnut Log. Rankin was murdered; Taylor escaped into swampland and was rescued the next day.

Governor Malcolm Patterson called in the Tennessee National Guard to quell the violence and identify and capture the Night Riders. By the end of October, almost one hundred alleged members of the group were assembled in a makeshift camp. Six of them were convicted and sentenced to death, but their conviction was over-turned by the state supreme court in 1909.

The Tennessee Historical Society recorded this infamous event as one of the most polarizing ones of West Tennessee, with neighbor pitted against neighbor in the region of Reelfoot Lake. As a result of the West Tennessee Land Company's greed and the subsequent Night Riders' violence, the state of Tennessee acquired the land in 1914, returning it to the people.

★ **J. Frank Dalton:** Also known as "Happy Jack," this man's real identity remains a mystery. While working at a carnival, he met Frank James, and Dalton appeared at the Tennessee State Fair in 1948 as Jesse James himself. His claims were supported by "Colonel" James Russell Davis. Debunked by some as a weaver of fantasy, Dalton circulated the story of the Confederate Underground, a group also known as the Knights of the Golden Circle, who reputedly were plotting for a second Civil War from their headquarters on Fatherland Street in Nashville. Dalton died in 1951.

★ **Jacob Franklin "Jake" Butcher:** With his brother Cecil Butcher Jr., Jake amassed a multibillion-dollar empire in the banking business in the 1970s and early 1980s, taking over Hamilton National Bank in Knoxville, whose name he changed to United American Bank.

Federal bank examiners began to suspect that the Butchers were moving their assets from one bank to another, making it seem as though they had more money than they did. The investigation proved the examiners right: they discovered a paper pyramid of bank fraud, unsecured loans, and forged documentation.

Jake Butcher, who had been a strong contender in a gubernatorial race, pleaded guilty to bank fraud charges in 1985. Although he was sentenced to twenty years' prison time, he only served seven and was released on parole in 1992.

Strange . . . but True

A Tragic Loss

Bob Riley was one of the first raft pilots to take large drifts of logs from Celina to Nashville on the upper Cumberland River in the late 1800s. It was a dangerous life, but he had many adventures and became a kind of folklore figure, full of tricks and mischief.

A popular story about Riley says that one night he stole a calf from a farmer and put it on his raft. Suspecting the farmer would come looking for his property, Riley dressed the animal in a raincoat and boots and had it lie down on the raft. Sure enough, along came the owner.

"I'm missing a calf," he said to Riley. "Have you seen one around?"

"A calf? Why, no," replied Riley.

The farmer looked at the prostrate calf, and in the darkness saw a figure lying there, dressed in raincoat and boots. "Who's that?"

"Oh." Riley looked downcast. "That is . . . was . . . my brother. He just died. Smallpox."

The owner took one step back from the raft, then two. "Sorry to hear that. I'll just keep on looking for my calf."

"You do that," Riley said above his grief.

Did You Know? The "battle of Athens" was a peacetime battle, fought by post–World War II veterans against a corrupt political ring believed to be attempting to rig the election of 1946. To force the sheriff, Pat Mansfield, to return confiscated ballot boxes, the veterans broke into the National Guard Armory, took weapons and ammunition, and, when the boxes were still not returned, opened fire on the deputies and blew up the front of the jail with dynamite. Although this was an embarrassment to many because of the negative national press it got, the battle of Athens came to be a source of pride among those who, returning home, found themselves fighting for their freedoms on their home turf.

A Tragedy within a Tragedy: When a Murder Victim's Family Pleaded for the Accused

Martin Luther King Jr. stood on the balcony of the Lorraine Motel in Memphis, waving to the people below. It was April 4, 1968, at the height of the Memphis sanitation strike, and he was there to support it as part of his Poor People's Campaign. He felt a sense of change in the air, but also of violence. Only the night before he had said, "I may not get there with you, but we as a people will make it to the promised land."

His words were eerily prophetic. A gunshot sounded and onlookers watched in horror as King fell dead, the victim of an assassin's bullet. Charged with the slaying was James Earl Ray, who was soon afterward arrested in London, England. He pleaded guilty to the shooting and was sentenced to ninety-nine years in prison. Until recently, that would have been the end of the story.

Ray, however, began to recant his guilty plea. First he told people he pleaded guilty because he had been framed with overwhelming evidence against him. He felt his family was threatened and feared for the death penalty. As the years dragged on, his incarceration seemed interminable. Then when Ray fell ill from liver disease, his pleas for a new trial and justice began to reach more and more people.

Some of those people included the family of Martin Luther King Jr., especially one of King's sons, who went to see Ray. In an extraordinary conversation in the Tennessee State Prison, Dexter King asked Ray, "Did you kill my father?"

Ray was near death and in need of a liver transplant. People in that kind of situation usually have little to hide. He looked King in the eyes and responded, "No, no, I didn't. No."

King's amazing response was, "I believe you and my family believes you. And we will do everything in our power to see you prevail."

Since then, Jerry Ray (James Earl Ray's brother), Dexter King, and Coretta Scott King (King's widow) have tried to have the case reopened and a more in-depth investigation done of the clues surrounding the assassination, including a more sophisticated ballistics test of the alleged murder weapon. The Reverend James Lawson, minister and stalwart civil rights leader who had invited King to come to Memphis to support the strike, asked for donations to pay for Ray's liver transplant. If he stayed alive, the

The Lorraine Motel in Memphis, where Dr. Martin Luther King Jr. was assassinated, was reopened as the National Civil Rights Museum in 1994. (COURTESY MEMPHIS CONVENTION & VISITORS BUREAU)

case would remain open. For a time, it seemed justice, or at least further investigation, had a chance.

In 1998 Attorney General Janet Reno ordered a limited investigation into allegations of a conspiracy in the King murder case. On April 23, 1998, James Earl Ray died of liver failure in Nashville Memorial Hospital, making a reopening of the case moot. It was thirty years and a few days after the death of Martin Luther King Jr.

In a poignant postscript, in December 1999 the Associated Press reported, "A jury hearing a lawsuit filed by [King's family] found that the civil rights leader was the victim of a vast murder conspiracy, not a lone assassin." On hearing this, Mike Gabriel, Ray's friend who was at his deathbed, said, "Dexter [King] has said this will rewrite history."

While we may never know the real truth behind King's assassination, this is one of the few times in American history that the family of a murder victim went to such great lengths to help the accused murderer attain justice.

James Earl Ray continued to protest his innocence, even when he was near death, and the family of his "victim," Martin Luther King Jr., agreed to fight for his retrial. This photo was taken in prison, shortly before his death. (COURTESY JERRY RAY)

The Alcatraz of Tennessee

Brushy Mountain State Penitentiary has held many famous and infamous inmates, including James Earl Ray. It also has a museum located on the grounds that is open by appointment. One of the artifacts is a ladder used by Ray for an escape attempt—said to have precipitated the largest manhunt ever in Tennessee.

Also worth a trip is the Franklin County Jail Museum, located in Winchester, with exhibits of Native American artifacts found in the area, Civil War memorabilia, and items from World Wars I and II. Capable of holding sixteen prisoners, the jail operated as such until the 1970s, with the sheriff and his family living upstairs.

The Infamous James Gang: A Few Odd Facts

★ **Jesse Woodson James:** During the 1870s a man calling himself John David Howard lived alternately in Nashville and in Humphreys County. When it was revealed that he was Jesse James, he fled the state with his brother Frank and their families. One story that portrays him and his brother as folk heroes claims they gave local African Americans the proceeds from a bank robbery to start a school.

★ **Alexander Franklin "Frank" James:** Lawrence County historical documents indicate that Frank James, Jesse's brother, settled in that county after the Civil War. They also point to the existence of a secret underground in post–Civil War Lawrence County that included over twenty-five hundred Confederate soldiers who did not surrender; Frank James was involved in this group's furtive activities. It's said he also taught school and lived a quiet, private life. Another story says, however, that Frank left Tennessee and joined Thomas Coleman Younger in an ill-fated attempt at a Wild West show. Either way, the people in Lawrenceburg can show you the (contested) grave site of Frank James.

★ **Thomas Coleman Younger:** Younger and Frank James went into partnership to produce a show like Buffalo Bill's highly successful one. Unfortunately, the James-Younger Wild West Show was a failure, and the crew never seemed to stay out of trouble. Younger is buried in Lee's Summit, Missouri.

★ **Jesse Edwards James:** Born in Nashville to outlaw Jesse and Zee James, Jesse Edwards James's story may be the most colorful of all the James Gang. His parents never told him his real name (his own alias was Tim Howard and sometimes Charlie) until after his father's death in 1882. He wrote the book *Jesse James, My Father* in 1899, became a lawyer, and starred in a silent movie in 1920 entitled *Jesse James under the Black Flag.* He portrayed his own father in the film.

★ **William Ryan and James Andrew "Dick" Liddil:** Ryan and Liddil were lesser-known members of the James Gang. Ryan was captured after the gang robbed trains in Missouri and Tennessee. He served time in prison (1881–89), then disappeared into obscurity following his release. Dick Liddil surrendered to legal agents in 1882, was pardoned, then worked as a tavern-keeper with Bob Ford, who took the credit for killing Jesse James.

The Day It Rained Snakes in Memphis

January 1877 was unusually cold, with ice hindering navigation on the rivers and bitter weather keeping most Tennesseans indoors. But it was in Memphis on January 15 that the weather took an unusual twist.

On that day, it began to rain, not just a gentle rain, but a torrential one. In the southern part of the city, though, they got more than just heavy rains. For some still-unexplained reason, not only did raindrops fall on their heads—so did snakes!

The phenomenon was contained within the space of a few city blocks, but it was more than just a handful of snakes. Thousands of dark, almost black, snakes, about a foot to a foot and a half in length, fell from the sky. So many snakes descended with the precipitation that several days later, there were still snakes on the ground.

The story garnered national attention. Even the *New York Times* mentioned it. However, no one has ever been able to offer a satisfactory explanation for the day it rained snakes.

A Mummy Story

Finis L. Bates was a lawyer in Memphis in the 1870s when he met a man in Texas who claimed to be Abraham Lincoln's assassin, John Wilkes Booth. Bates later identified a suicide victim in 1903 as the same man, although the man had been an actor going by the name of David E. George. Bates had the body embalmed, stored it in his garage in Memphis, and wrote a book, *The Escape and Suicide of John Wilkes Booth*, which sold seventy thousand copies when it came out in 1907.

After Bates's death in 1923, the "mummy" became a sideshow exhibit in a carnival and was last seen at a fair in New Hope, Pennsylvania, in 1975. Since its disappearance, a Memphis man named Ken Hawkes has been avidly searching for the mummy to settle once and for all the question of its identity.

This quirky bit of history has become legendary and has been featured on NBC's *Unsolved Mysteries* and ABC's *20/20*. Publications such as *Life, The Saturday Evening Post,* and *Rolling Stone* have run stories about the mystery as well.

The mummy's whereabouts are currently unknown, but if you find it, please call Ken.

Strange . . . but True

The Knoxville-born author and journalist James Agee died in an automobile accident on May 16, 1955—thirty-nine years to the day after his own father died, also in an automobile accident.

The Professor Who Spontaneously Combusted

People have been known to just catch on fire, and a professor in Nashville lived to tell about it.

The phenomenon of spontaneous human combustion (SHC) is one that has been observed but never satisfactorily explained. According to various scientific accounts, it begins in the victim with a "small jet of flame," which spreads quite rapidly over the whole body. The fire is intense, one account saying, "in excess of 3,000 degrees Fahrenheit." Because of this intensity, if water is thrown onto a burning victim, the hydrogen and oxygen molecules, which are highly volatile, separate and increase the fire's intensity.

Such was the experience of James Hamilton, a thin, soft-spoken professor of mathematics, astronomy, and natural philosophy at the University of Nashville, in 1835. Professor Hamilton gave a lecture to his students on January 5, then walked home in eight-degree weather for his noon break.

Arriving home, Dr. Hamilton recorded the barometric and temperature readings for the day, then went outside to check his hygrometer so he could note the speed and direction of the cold January wind. That's when the unimaginable happened. Feeling a sharp, intense pain on, not in, his left leg, Dr. Hamilton slapped at it. This only made it worse. The pain grew more intense, and Hamilton pulled up his pants leg to see what was causing him such extreme discomfort.

He was amazed to see a small flame about the diameter of a dime shooting out of his leg! Thinking quickly, Hamilton put his hands over the flame and the absence of oxygen caused the fire to die out. There remained a large burn on his skin—but what further amazed Hamilton is that his clothing was intact. Hamilton tried to treat the unusual burn with salves and finally went to see Dr. John Overton, who diagnosed his case as spontaneous human combustion.

Virtually all medical and scientific records maintain that people die almost immediately from SHC, because they become engulfed in flames so rapidly. Without Hamilton's quick thinking, he would have been added to the number of people who die in such a bizarre fashion.

When the Fish Hits the Pan, or Gentlemen, Start Your Fins

Every April at the annual World's Largest Fish Fry in Paris, Tennessee, an unusual racing event is held. On the lawn of the Paris courthouse, using a fifteen-foot-long Plexiglas trough of water for a track, the Parisians hold a catfish race.

I still don't know: does the winning fish get to choose whether it's deep-fat or pan fried?

Where Lawyers, Politicians, and Preachers Can't Compete!

The Middle Tennessee town of Dickson has its own special event, and it's located in a rather weird spot. Since 1959, every April they have a Liar's Contest in the building formerly known as the Grand Ole Hatchery. The hatchery was once the nation's fifth largest chicken hatchery, but it now is devoted to music, comedy, and other entertainment, when it's not filled with liars.

Trying to maintain an amateur character, the Liar's Contest bars politicians, lawyers, and preachers. Otherwise there are no rules. One of the locals put it this way: "We do have some standards, but over the years we have gotten rid of most of them."

An Elephant Who Was Executed

Once upon a time an execution in the Volunteer State was of elephantine proportions: the hanging of an elephant called "Murderous Mary."

Mary was owned by the Sparks Brothers Circus, who had come to perform in the East Tennessee town of Kingsport. She was proclaimed to be "the largest living land animal on earth" and was said to weigh more than five tons. Mary was being attended by her temporary trainer, Walter Eldridge, when she made a lunge for the lemonade stand. When Eldridge made an attempt to restrain the pachyderm by hitting her with his club, Mary lost her temper, picked up the hapless trainer, and killed him. Some accounts say she trampled him; others say she dashed him on the ground. Either way, Eldridge was dead.

The people of Kingsport felt they had to avenge Eldridge's death, and according to one account, some kind of trial was held. The circus owner agreed to the death penalty; apparently, he was nearby when Mary grabbed her victim, and it could have been him. First they tried to shoot her, but no bullet could pierce Mary's tough hide; so she was taken to nearby Erwin, the headquarters of Clinchfield Railroad, to be hanged from a railroad derrick.

After her weight broke the first chain around her neck, the handlers were successful with a stronger one, and Mary hung by the neck until she was dead, witnessed by between two hundred and five thousand people, depending on which account you read. A steam shovel was used to dig Mary's grave and bury her on the spot. Accounts of the hanging were published in such magazines as *Tennessee Conservationist, Argosy, Popular Mechanics,* and *Ripley's Believe It or Not.* Whether or not there was a trial, the hanging remains the most bizarre one ever to have occurred in the United States.

After killing her trainer, Mary the elephant was hanged from a railroad derrick in Erwin. (COURTESY THE *ERWIN RECORD*)

Eerie Goings-on in Chapel Hill

It seems just about every part of Tennessee has its "ghost light." There's one in Elora and one in Big South Fork country, but the best-known one is in Chapel Hill, just northwest of Shelbyville. The story of exactly when the phenomenon began is unclear, but any resident of the town could tell you the folklore behind it.

Long ago a signalman along the Louisville and Nashville Railroad line went out on a dark and rainy night to inspect the line of track. This was part of his often thankless job. With his lantern held high, he set out to make his inspection before the express train came through. The stories vary at this point, but somehow the signalman was struck and killed by the speeding night train; all the man's bodily parts were recovered except for—you guessed it—his head.

Now no one can say exactly when Chapel Hill became an unwilling host to "the ghost of the tracks," but it has been spotted by a number of Chapel Hill residents and visitors. It comes down the line in a kind of bobbing motion, as if the track is being inspected. Christopher K. Coleman wrote in his book *Strange Tales of the Dark and Bloody Ground* (Nashville: Rutledge Hill Press, 1998), "Next to the Bell Witch . . . the Chapel Hill Ghost Light is the most noted unexplained phenomenon in Tennessee—and among the most famous in the South." Whatever has caused it, the Ghost Light of Chapel Hill still defies explanation.

Tennessee's Form of "Montezuma's Revenge"

In 1540 when Hernando DeSoto visited the Cherokee village of Canasoga in what is now Polk County, about twenty of the villagers brought his expedition a little "welcome gift." Each carried a basket of mulberries. This may be the first time in Tennessee that whites experienced a form of Montezuma's Revenge.

No Smoking, but Hard Drugs Are Okay

In 1897 Governor Robert Taylor signed a bill that banned cigarettes from the Volunteer State, making it a misdemeanor for "any person, firm or corporation to sell, or to bring into the State for the purpose of selling, giving away or otherwise disposing of cigarettes, [or] cigarette papers." Although that law was overturned in 1900 during Governor Benton McMillin's administration, the unauthorized sale of cocaine, morphine, heroin, or opium was not made illegal until 1913.

One Grisly Tale

It was dark as pitch when Captain James W. Davis rode on horseback through the territory near McMinnville on the night of March 16, 1882. The revenue agent was known for his extraordinary ability to "sniff out" illegal moonshine stills. He had a reputation for being able to follow a trail as well as any Cherokee, Creek, or Chickasaw, and he could stay in the saddle without sleep or respite, for days on end.

Davis had been traveling a great deal since he'd become a revenue agent after the Civil War. The state governments of Tennessee, Georgia, and North Carolina, as well as the U.S. government, had often employed him to find and bring down the makers of moonshine and their illicit whiskey operations. He'd made a lot of enemies in the years he'd spent riding against the still operations, having arrested more than three thousand people and destroyed nearly seven hundred stills. But he also had friends in high places throughout the region.

On this night neither Davis's reputation nor his luck would save him. At least ten moonshiners were hidden in some brush when he rode by, and they set upon Davis with a vengeance. He was killed in a hail of crossfire.

Despite the high number of attackers, not one local person seemed to have a clue as to who the perpetrators could be. His murder is still unsolved.

 # TRULY BIZARRE TRIVIA

Q. Into what animal-related partnership did Jesse James enter with a member of his gang, Edward Miller?

A. They bought a racehorse named *Jim Malone*. (It is suspected that James murdered his partner in an argument over the horse in the summer of 1880.)

Q. In Memphis in 1879, an ordinance was pending that prohibited the smoking of what particular substance?

A. Opium. (The editor of the *Memphis Public Ledger* wrote a protest in response.)

Q. Who was the original Grand Wizard and chief officer of the Ku Klux Klan?

A. General Nathan Bedford Forrest.

Q. What bizarre item did Jeremiah George Harris bring back as a gift to the Tennessee Historical Society when he returned from his travels with the U.S. Navy in 1860?

A. A mummy from Egypt. The mummy is still on display in the Tennessee State Museum, Nashville.

Q. What actor, who later committed a heinous murder, gave a benefit performance in Nashville in 1864?

A. John Wilkes Booth. (Ironically, his final performance was on February 12, the birthday of the president he assassinated fourteen months later.)

2

Politics and Transportation

Politics Makes Strange Bedfellows

Tennessee politicians have always had a special air about them, something that sets them apart from politicians in the rest of the country. They have the swagger of what has been called a "frontier democrat," showing, with flannel shirt sleeves rolled up, that they are just one of the people. Two of Tennessee's more flamboyant politicians who ran against each other happened to be brothers.

Robert Love Taylor (born 1850) and Alf Taylor (born 1848) were born and raised in Happy Valley in Carter County. They enjoyed the rough-and-tumble antics and friendly fights any other brothers might have had, and then some, because they learned early on how to be at odds by their parents' example. Their father, Nathaniel G. Taylor, had been affiliated with the Whigs in northeastern Tennessee. Their mother, Emmeline Hayes Taylor, had a brother (Landon C. Hayes), who'd served as senator from Tennessee in the Congress of the Confederate States of America. To her, most likely, the War of Northern Aggression and Southern Rebellion was not really ended. Thus was the home environment in which Bob and Alf Taylor were raised.

Alf grew up to become affiliated with the Republican Party; Bob went with the Democrats. When each decided to run for Governor in 1886, the situation attracted the imaginations of the people and the media.

Brothers Bob (left) and Alf Taylor competed against each other in the 1886 race for the office of governor. (COURTESY TENNESSEE STATE MUSEUM PHOTOGRAPHIC ARCHIVES)

Naming their political competition the "War of the Roses" after the fifteenth-century struggle for the English crown, Alf Taylor's Republicans wore red roses and Bob's Democratic supporters wore white. Their political stumping was amicable for the most part: they oftentimes shared not only a hotel room but the bed, as well. And, like so many politicians who are of a musical bent, Bob and Alf even got into a fiddling contest during their campaign of 1886.

When it came voting time, Bob won by a landslide victory of more than thirteen thousand votes. Undaunted, however, Alf persisted—and also became governor when he was seventy-two, in the gubernatorial election of 1921.

Today Bob and Alf Taylor, the brothers who once shared a hotel room and bed while campaigning against each other, share a burial plot in Elizabethtown, Carter County, in front of the Franklin Club.

Bare-Faced Honest (Along with Everything Else)

In 1966 a Knoxville panel consisting of three federal judges ruled a certain state law unconstitutional. The law was challenged by the American

Sunbathing Association and the Tennessee Outdoor Club, because it tried to do away with nudist camps in Tennessee. Thus nudist camps are still legal in Tennessee.

Sam Houston: A Tennessean Who Paid His Debts

Samuel Houston was not originally a Tennessean. Born near Lexington, Virginia, in 1793, Sam was the middle child of nine. After his father's death and the sale of their Virginia home, his mother took her large brood to a farm near Maryville, Tennessee.

Houston was impatient to learn all he could about everything and was an avid reader. To help support his family, he worked a while in a store in Maryville owned by a Mr. Weber, but he couldn't take being indoors. Leaving with only some food, his books, and a musket, Houston ran away. For three years he lived with the Cherokee in their village on Hiwassee Island (in the middle of the Hiwassee River), and there he learned to live in the natural rhythms of the native people. After some time with them, he could run twenty-five miles in a day alongside the best braves and hunt with a bow and arrow. Finally, the chief of the village gave Sam Houston an Indian name: *Co-lon-eh*, meaning "the Raven," one of the Cherokees' favorite birds.

In a spirit of gratitude, the Raven returned to Weber's store in Maryville to buy gifts for his new friends. He paid for the gifts with two deerskins and paper on which he scrawled, "IOU $35.00. Sam Houston." Several times he returned to the store, adding to the debt each time. "I'll pay the debt," he always said.

Finally Mr. Weber refused to let Houston charge anything else. "By now, you owe me one hundred dollars!" he declared.

"Injun Sam," as local settlers called him, was perplexed: he fully intended to pay the debt but was uncertain how he could do it right away. In town with his family a few weeks later, Sam entered a spelling bee and won. When someone said, "You should be a teacher," Sam decided to do just that.

He opened his school in an empty log cabin in Maryville, which was soon full of students. In this way he began to pay off what he owed Mr. Weber.

Destiny had Sam Houston going on to become a soldier, lawyer, congressman, and governor of both Tennessee and Texas. Fighting for Texas's independence from Mexico, Houston led his men to a victory in the battle of San Jacinto. Houston then became president of the Republic of Texas. After Texas became a state in 1844, he served as a U.S. Senator. Tennessee-raised Sam Houston is the only senator who also was the president of another country.

Although there are other monuments to him, a log schoolhouse near Maryville, where he was a teacher in his early years, is a monument to one who was not Tennessee-born but had Tennessee pride in his veins—pride that made him pay his debts.

Cities and Their Nicknames

Can you match these Tennessee cities with their nicknames? (Hint: Some of the cities have more than one nickname.)

City	Nickname
1. Chattanooga	A. Bluff City
2. Clarksville	B. Music City
3. Memphis	C. Jewel of the Cumberland
4. Nashville	D. Athens of the South
5. Shelbyville	E. Queen City
	G. Pencil City (in the 1950s)
	F. Chicago of the South

Answers: 1. (F)   2. (C, E)   3. (A)   4. (B, D)   5. (G)

An Accused Murderer and the Victim's Widow Share a Ballot

Cookeville is a serene, clean town in north-central Tennessee, where generally, peace and respect prevail.

The peaceful atmosphere was shattered October 19, 1998, when Senator Tommy Burks was shot on his farm, which straddles the Cumberland-Putnam County line. He was fifty-eight years old and said to be a friend of the farmer, the downtrodden, the abused, the victims of crime; many decried the irony of Burks himself becoming a victim of violence. Most people couldn't envision anyone having a grudge against Burks.

In the fifteenth senatorial district race, Burks's death left one candidate remaining on the ballot: Byron "Low Tax" Looper, the controversial tax assessor of Putnam County. Looper was a Republican; Burks had been a Democrat. Now Burks's grieving friends sought to find someone to be a write-in candidate against Looper.

But anyone who read the papers would have doubted Looper's character. A grand jury had charged him with fourteen counts of theft and misuse of office. He had also had a paternity suit filed against him by a former girlfriend, an exotic dancer. Looper had legally adopted his middle name, Low Tax, no doubt thinking it would help his political career. As friends gave Burks their final respects, investigators worked to solve his murder and ultimately charged Looper with the killing.

The irony—that the person accused of murdering a politician was himself a candidate for the same office as his alleged victim—increased when Burks's widow, Charlotte, won the senate seat in a last-minute write-in campaign. On August 23, 2000, Byron Looper was convicted of first-degree murder and sentenced to life imprisonment without possibility of parole. His lawyers vowed to appeal.

Death for Defending First Amendment Rights

Alone at the end of the workday in his newspaper office, Edward Carmack toyed with the handle of his Smith and Wesson as he contemplated the possibility of his own death. Little did he realize on the afternoon of November 9, 1908, that this would be one of the last possibilities he would ever entertain.

Born in 1858 in Sumner County, Carmack has always been outspoken, sometimes even vindictive, self-righteous, and passionate in his beliefs. With

Edward Carmack, editor of the Nashville Tennessean, died defending the right of freedom of the press. (COURTESY TENNESSEE STATE LIBRARY AND ARCHIVES)

this attitude, he began to have troubles early on. He was suspended from the highly acclaimed Webb School in Bell Buckle for taunting a fellow student in a religious dispute; Carmack then took up the study of law instead of the classics that had been taught at his former alma mater.

Growing up in the time of crisis between the North and the South, Carmack witnessed much of the Civil War and Reconstruction and began to keep a journal. This journalistic bent would stay with him the rest of his tragically brief life.

Edward Carmack had a number of interests. He established a law practice in Columbia, and for a time was editor in chief of both the *Nashville Democrat* and the *Memphis Commercial Appeal*, as well as other smaller newspapers. He also served in the state legislature, the U.S. House of Representatives, and the U.S. Senate. He had high hopes to be chosen as the Democratic gubernatorial candidate during its 1907 convention, but to his dismay, Malcolm Patterson, someone with whom he politically disagreed, won the nod. Ultimately, his passions for both politics and journalism would lead to his death.

While Patterson was campaigning for governor of Tennessee in 1907,

Carmack was editor of the Nashville *Tennessean*. Using his newspaper as a forum, Carmack voiced negative opinions about a future Patterson administration with its ties to a political machine, and denounced saloons and the use of liquor in any form.

As governor, Patterson had an enemy in Carmack, but the governor had an ally named Colonel Duncan Cooper, who had plans to defeat the proposed prohibition of liquor. The colonel and his son Robin threatened to harm Carmack if he wrote any further editorials against Patterson, his cronies, and the liquor trade.

Although he didn't want to believe the Coopers would do any real violence to him, Carmack nonetheless began carrying his Smith and Wesson revolver. One day he found himself in need of it.

After he left his office and headed for home on November 9, 1908, he stopped near the intersection of Seventh Avenue and Union Street to chat with two ladies of his acquaintance. The Coopers accosted him, and the moment Carmack had feared was upon him. There was no time to aim and shoot carefully. Four shots rang out, the women screamed, and Robin Cooper walked away, slightly wounded, with his father's help. The outspoken editor of the *Tennessean* was dead with three bullets in his body.

Edward Carmack now lies buried in a cemetery in Columbia, but his statue stands on the capitol grounds. Both Coopers, father and son, were tried, found guilty of murder, and each sentenced to twenty years in prison. Through appellate procedures, the duo was later freed: Robin, on a technicality, and Duncan, by a pardon from Governor Patterson. Colonel Cooper died in his bed in 1922; his son Robin, however, was murdered in 1919 by unknown killer(s).

Carmack died exercising his right of freedom of the press under the First Amendment to the Constitution. Editors who wrote his eulogies, however, while praising him for his high and unbending standards, agreed with what the *Memphis Commercial Appeal* wrote: "His pen was too often steeped in bitterness . . ."

Did he die defending the First Amendment? Or did he ultimately die by his own "poisoned pen"?

Strange . . . but True

One Bad Editor and One Poor Marksman

In Knoxville on March 11, 1882, an encounter similar to Carmack's occurred, but with results much less tragic—in fact, it was nearly comical. James Walker, editor of the *Knoxville Tribune*, encountered his rival, William Rule, editor of the *Knoxville Chronicle*, near the corner of Gay and Church Streets. Walker had, as they say, "a bone to pick."

He demanded to know if it was true that Rule had written something insulting about him, and Rule replied yes, he had. "I demand an apology!" Walker announced. Instead, Rule began to strike Walker with his cane. Drawing his revolver, Walker shot at Rule, who first fell to the ground, then got up and fled to a nearby apothecary.

Walker sought out the sheriff and gave himself up. When he was released on bond, he discovered that his bullets hadn't even struck Rule; the editor had merely suffered from powder burns and had probably fallen down in fright.

Tennessee and the Perfect Thirty-six

Anne Dallas Dudley (Mrs. Guilford Dudley) was the envy of every socially ambitious woman in Nashville. Prominent, respected, and wealthy, Anne Dudley was also one of Tennessee's first suffragettes. In the summer of 1920 she was actively campaigning for women's right to vote.

The nation's attention was on Tennessee that year. Thirty-five states had already ratified what would become the Nineteenth Amendment, and ratification by only one more state was needed for it to become law. The Tennessee General Assembly was in session to consider having the state become "the perfect thirty-six."

Anne Dudley was right in the middle of things: she traveled throughout Tennessee, speaking to people about her vision of when "a woman's home will be the whole world" and urged Tennessee congressmen to vote for the amendment. She was scoffed at and ridiculed by the press and much of the public . . . that is, until her cause became more popular and even women who had no interest in voting began to support their choice to do so.

Another "War of the Roses" broke out in Tennessee that hot summer. Women who were for the amendment wore yellow roses and ribbons, and those who opposed it wore red. As time passed, more young ladies' and matrons' blouses were decorated with yellow than scarlet.

Due in large part to Anne Dallas Dudley's efforts, Tennessee ratified the Nineteenth Amendment in August 1920, making women's suffrage the law of the land and furthering American women in their battle for equality of the sexes.

Did You Know? The first black man to hold judicial posts in the city of Nashville, and the first to hold the position of supreme court justice of Tennessee, was Adolpho A. Birch. He was Nashville's first black assistant attorney general (1966), was the first black judge appointed to be in charge of General Sessions Court in the city (1969), and was named criminal court judge by Governor Ray Blanton (1978). He was appointed to the Tennessee Supreme Court in 1993.

Why Lamar Alexander Was Sworn In Early

January 7, 1979, was cold, dreary, and wet. Lamar Alexander and his wife, Honey, were preparing to move from their home in the Green Hills section of Nashville. Half of their possessions would go to their retreat in East Tennessee; the rest were being moved to the governor's mansion. Lamar Alexander was scheduled to be inaugurated January 10.

But Alexander would be sworn in early as Tennessee's governor. As Alexander sat writing his inaugural address, U.S. Attorney Hal Hardin telephoned him and came right to the point. Outgoing Governor Ray Blanton was about to release prisoners from the state penitentiary and Hardin suspected they had bought their freedom. To stop this from happening, Alexander had to take office immediately.

Alexander suggested that Hardin confer with some state leaders, including Lieutenant Governor John Wilder and State House Speaker Ned Ray McWherter, to get their thoughts on what was essentially a takeover. Although Wilder disapproved, saying the early swearing-in was unconstitutional, the general consensus was for Alexander to be inaugurated early.

Several hours later, wearing borrowed clothes because everything they owned had been moved during the day, Lamar, Honey, and their children were ready for the impromptu inauguration.

They piled into state trooper Herschel Winstead's unmarked car with their friend Tom Ingram and drove to the basement parking garage of the Supreme Court Building. Exiting an elevator, the Alexander family was enveloped by swarms of reporters, friends, and staff members. No one had been told what was going to happen; they had just been told to come.

Lamar Alexander took the oath of office surrounded by his friends and family. As he had written in his notes following Hardin's fateful call, he took office early because it was "in the best interests of the people of Tennessee."

Former Governor Ray Blanton was eventually convicted on charges relating to his unscrupulous activities and was imprisoned at Maxwell Air Force Base for twenty-two months. He died on November 22, 1996.

Hail to the (Vertically Challenged) Chief!

The tune "Hail to the Chief" was first played at the inauguration ceremony of Martin Van Buren in 1837. Sarah Childress Polk, however, is said to be the person responsible for the tune being played every time the president enters a room. She started this during the presidency of her husband, James K. Polk, the Tennessean who served from 1845 to 1849.

President Polk was only five feet, six inches tall. As a result, his entry often went unnoticed, and this annoyed Sarah. She had the White House band play "Hail to the Chief" so everyone in the room would know when President Polk arrived.

Every president since then (vertically challenged or not) has continued this musical tradition. The song itself has an interesting history. James Sanderson, an English composer, set the words from Sir Walter Scott's 1810 poem "The Lady of the Lake" to a traditional Scottish tune; he published the song in the United States in 1812. Here are the words so you can sing along:

Hail to the Chief

Hail to the Chief we have chosen for the na-tion,
Hail to the Chief! We salute him, one and all.
Hail to the Chief, as we pledge co-op-er-a-tion
In proud fulfillment of a great, noble call.
Yours is the aim to make this country grand-er,
This you will do, that's our strong, firm belief.
Hail to the one we selected as com-mander,
Hail to the Pres-i-dent! Hail to the Chief!
(Words by Sir Walter Scott, music by James Sanders)

Strange . . . but True

Shape Is Everything

Warren County, originally comprising nine hundred square miles, found itself shrinking as counties were formed around it. When the Tennessee State Constitution of 1834 ruled on boundaries and county seats, Warren County took on a distinctive shape.

The ruling said that when a new county was formed, the county seat had to be at least twelve miles from the county seat of the existing county. Therefore, with the creation of Grundy, Van Buren, Cannon, Coffee, and DeKalb Counties, Warren County became nearly perfectly round. It still has the nickname, "the Round County."

POLITICAL TRIVIA

Q. Who is the first Tennessee governor to serve two consecutive four-year terms of office?

A. Lamar Alexander.

Q. In 1920 Kingsport passed what bill to clean up the streets—literally?

A. The city's first antipollution ordinance, by which pigs were forbidden to roam the streets and were to be "removed from backyards."

Q. What colonel in the Confederate States of America and member of the Tennessee General Assembly and U.S. Congress was instrumental in removing federal troops from the beleaguered South and is buried in Henry County?

A. John DeWitt Clinton Atkins, 1825–1908.

Q. What Reconstruction-era governor of Tennessee was by trade a Methodist circuit rider and editor of the *Knoxville Whig?*

A. William G. "Parson" Brownlow.

Q. What trapper, soldier, and explorer served in the Tennessee General Assembly and the U.S. House of Representatives before dying at the Alamo in 1836?

A. David Crockett.

Q. On what day was the city of Nashville founded?

A. Christmas Day 1779.

Q. What man, known for his oratory skills, built a home in Clarksville known as Emerald Hill, served in the Tennessee and Kentucky legislatures, and was a senator in the Congress of the Confederate States?

A. Gustavus Adolphus Henry, the "Eagle Orator of Tennessee."

Q. What antebellum home near Nashville was built by the seventh president of the United States, who is buried on its grounds?

A. The Hermitage, home of Andrew Jackson.

Q. As a result of the elections of 1966, what U.S. senator was the first popularly elected GOP senator in Tennessee's history and the first Republican to win a statewide election since 1920?

A. Howard H. Baker Jr.

Q. Senator Howard Baker Sr. refused to sign what racist document, which protested the U.S. Supreme Court's decision in the case *Brown v. Board of Education* (1954)?

A. The "Southern Manifesto."

Q. Because of his role in founding the United Nations, what Tennessee-born former U.S. senator and secretary of state received the Nobel Peace Prize in 1945?

A. Cordell Hull.

Q. What Tennessean was the first U.S. president to be impeached?

A. Andrew Johnson.

Q. Before turning to politics, Andrew Johnson followed what business?

A. Tailoring. (His first shop is in Rutledge, Grainger County.)

Q. Who was the first African American to serve in the Tennessee General Assembly?

A. Sampson W. Keeble.

Q. In 1973 what object did Congressman Dan Kuykendall (R-Tenn.) hold up to dramatize his entreaty against the U.S. House of Representatives' rushing to begin impeachment proceedings against President Richard M. Nixon?

A. A hangman's noose, warning them not to become a "legislative lynch mob."

Q. During the fight for women's suffrage, the groups both for and against it stayed at what famous Nashville hotel?

A. Hermitage.

Q. Between what state and what nation was the Treaty of Dumplin County signed in Sevier County in 1785?

A. The State of Franklin, represented by Major Hugh Henry, and the Cherokee Nation, represented by Ancoo, chief of the Chota, allowing settlement in the area between the Holston and French Broad Rivers.

Q. By what dramatic action did Lamar Alexander campaign for governor in 1978?

A. Walking across the state—1,022 miles.

Q. Who was the first African American surgeon in the Southeast and the first African American woman elected to the Tennessee General Assembly?

A. Dorothy Lavinia Brown.

Q. In 1958 what environmentally conscious U.S. senator from Tennessee recommended to President Dwight D. Eisenhower that he stop exploding nuclear weapons in the atmosphere for three years?

A. Al Gore Sr., father of Vice President Al Gore Jr.

Q. Who was the first African American to run for governor of Tennessee?

A. William Francis Yardley, in 1876.

Q. During the Civil War the U.S. Army Medical Corps legalized what controversial social practice?

A. Prostitution, to protect soldiers from disease, by legalizing the "trade."

Q. In 1869 "Radical Republican" state senator Philip Nelson introduced a bill to allow women to wear what type of clothing?

A. Pants, for more freedom of movement. (The bill states: "Be it enacted, etc., That the costume now worn by female citizens of Tennessee be changed from petticoats to pants. . . .")

Q. What three U.S. presidents came from Tennessee?

A. Andrew Jackson, Andrew Johnson, and James K. Polk.

Q. In 1772 James Robertson and John Sevier established what self-governing community in eastern Tennessee?

A. Watauga Settlers Association.

Q. In 1839 how many Cherokee were in Tennessee when their infamous forced march to Oklahoma began?

A. Around fifteen thousand men, women, and children. (Around four thousand died along "the Trail of Tears.")

Q. Who was the first governor of Tennessee?

A. John Sevier.

Q. In 1682 Tennessee was claimed for what country?

A. France, by Pierre Cavelier, Sieur de La Salle.

Q. What is the smallest county in Tennessee?

A. Trousdale, in northern Middle Tennessee, nicknamed "the runt of the state."

Q. How many Republican governors has Tennessee had between 1900 and 2000?

A. Five (Ben Hooper, Alfred Taylor, Winfield Dunn, Lamar Alexander, and Don Sundquist).

Q. William Carroll served how many terms as governor of Tennessee?

A. Six (it's a record).

Q. The first "dark-horse" candidate to win a presidential nomination was which Tennessean?

A. James K. Polk.

Q. What Tennessee commissioner of education from 1963 to 1971, who was known as a "bare-knuckled political brawler," dominated Lewis County politics during his lifetime?

A. John Howard Warf (1904–1996).

Q. What were President Andrew Jackson's last words?

A. "We shall all meet in heaven."

Did You Know? At one time, the Louisville and Nashville Railroad had competition for its use of Union Station in Nashville. The Tennessee Central Railroad, founded by Jere Baxter, built a line that reached into previously inaccessible areas of Tennessee. The line was the major link to the outside world for many because of Baxter's efforts—but he failed in his attempts to wrest total control of Union Station from the L&N.

Lawrence County: Home of Aviation's Pioneer?

Soon after the Civil War, James Jackson Pennington of Henryville began making sketches of his "flying machine." His aeronautical wonder consisted of a balloon under which was suspended a fan, which drew air into a chamber and expelled it though a narrow opening, causing the machine to fly. In a letter to a friend, Pennington claimed, "My aerial bird had the power to . . . cross the briny deepe [*sic*] and plane the North Pole and conquer the world and will stop all Wars."

Originally it was about the size of a mouse trap, but Pennington continued to tinker with his machine, making it ever larger, until it could carry a book weighing several pounds. He patented it through the U.S. Patent Office in 1877. Still trying to convince the general public of the reality of air transportation, he exhibited his "aerial bird" at the Columbia Exposition in Louisville, Kentucky, in 1883 and was offered money for his invention by two mysterious unidentified men. Pennington would not sell it to them.

After his death in 1885, two mysterious unidentified men came to Henryville and visited with Pennington's widow. After she died, the Pennington daughters sought to find their father's plans of the "aerial bird," but although they located the patent in the U.S. Patent Office, the plans were missing.

The family believes that Mrs. Pennington sold the plans to those two well-dressed visitors. It was in 1903 that a plane did get constructed and take flight, but it wasn't in Lawrence County, or even in Tennessee. Two brothers by the name of Orville and Wilbur Wright made their historic flight in North Carolina.

Had the Wright brothers purchased those plans from Mrs. Pennington? Or were her two visitors aviation pioneers from Paris, France, as some suggested? It remains an unsolved mystery, but whatever the truth is in regard to Pennington and his plans, Pennington Field, the airfield in Henryville, carries his name in honor of his contribution to aviation.

Did You Know? The first B-17 bomber to complete twenty-five missions over Europe in World War II and return to the U.S. under its own power was the *Memphis Belle,* now on permanent display at Memphis's Mud Island. The plane and its crew were the subject of a feature film entitled *Memphis Belle.*

For Railroad Buffs

Billed as "The Largest Operating Historic Railroad in the South," the Tennessee Valley Railroad Museum is located in Chattanooga. It was started in 1959 as a way to preserve the era of steam locomotion and passenger

Trains of the Tennessee Valley Railroad offer daily rides from Chattanooga, some with a dining car luncheon onboard. (COURTESY TENNESSEE VALLEY RAILROAD; PHOTO BY STEVEN R. FREER)

trains. The museum consists of an active restoration workshop where engines dating back to the 1900s and beyond are repaired and restored. In the train yard itself there is a working turntable, train depot (the East Chattanooga Station), and the museum inside the terminal. Regular six-mile train rides and special excursions are offered throughout the year.

Another interesting museum is located in Jackson, Tennessee: Casey Jones Village, which is dedicated to the courage and memory of "the brave engineer." Check out his story in Chapter 4, "Famous Tennesseans."

The Building of "the World's Steepest Passenger Railway"

In the latter part of the nineteenth century, people liked to come to Chattanooga in the summer months to enjoy the mountain elevation and the relatively cool climate it offered. For the alert entrepreneurs in Chattanooga, easy access to Lookout Mountain for these visitors would mean increased revenues for themselves and the city.

Two attempts at maintaining and establishing rail service to the top of Lookout Mountain had not gone well. Then a Chattanoogan by the name of John T. Crass came up with the idea of an incline railway that would take passengers directly to the summit from a station at the base of the mountain. He formed the Lookout Mountain Incline Railway Company and set out to build the steepest, most direct route up the mountainside.

The first car ascended on November 16, 1895, and the Incline Railway could claim to be the steepest passenger railway in the world, with a grade of 72.7 percent at its steepest point. Named both a National Historic Site and a National Historic Mechanical Engineering Landmark, for over one hundred years it has taken millions of visitors up and down one of the most famous mountains in the world.

Hey, This Is Tennessee!
There's Got to Be a Section on Trucks!

In Chattanooga in 1998, a group identified as "Friends of Towing" opened the International Towing and Recovery Museum. Why Chattanooga? Because the world's first tow truck was made there in 1916. The museum has over 20 antique tow trucks and its hall of fame immortalizes manufacturers of tow trucks, more than 170 tow-truck drivers, and others who have had an international impact on the industry.

Antique tow trucks can be seen at the International Towing and Recovery Museum in Chattanooga. (COURTESY INTERNATIONAL TOWING AND RECOVERY MUSEUM; PHOTO BY MARK MARTIN)

The "Impossible" Tunnel

When there was a desire to offer rail service between Nashville and Chattanooga, the problem was how to get over the imposing Cumberland Plateau. Then Gerald Troost, Tennessee's first geologist, made a suggestion: if the railroad engineers couldn't see a way over the mountain, why not bore a hole through it? He suggested a tunnel through the portion of the rocky ridge of the Cumberland Mountains located near Cowan, Tennessee. In 1848 the N&C engineers decided his idea was worth a try.

It was an arduous and dangerous process. First, they made five simultaneous digs on the top of the mountain, chiseling three shafts from the mountain top down to tunnel level 170 feet below. The workers hacked away at the mountain, aided only by the light from torches, using picks, shovels, hand drills, and sledge hammers. Every day for three years, using round-the-clock laborers, the work progressed until the three shafts had reached tunnel level. Then the workers divided into two crews, fanning out in opposite directions, and dug and hacked their way until they saw sunlight. The tunnel was completed in 1852. It was 2,228 feet long.

Incorporated in 1845, the N&C was the first successful railroad line completed in Tennessee, reaching Chattanooga by 1854. The N&C Railroad became the nucleus for the Nashville, Chattanooga and St. Louis line, which formed in 1873 and is today part of the CSX line.

Apparently it's a mistake to tell a Tennessean, "You can't do that!"

> *Did You Know?* The LeGrange and Memphis Railroad was the first to operate in the state. It ran in 1842 but went bankrupt shortly afterwards.

 ## TRANSPORTATION TRIVIA

Q. How did Brownsville-born adventurer and author Richard Halliburton die in 1939?

A. In a storm while trying to cross the Pacific Ocean in his Chinese junk, the *Sea Dragon*.

Q. What was Tennessee's first official road?

A. Walton Road, named for William Walton, from Knoxville through Kingston to Nashville.

Q. What is Walton Road's highway designation today?

A. U.S. 70.

Q. In 1787 what delayed construction of Walton Road?

A. Indian fighting by the militia that had been called out to cut the wagon road.

Q. Where did the first section of interstate open in Tennessee in November 1958?

A. Ardmore, in Giles County, at the interchange of the Alabama border.

Q. In what city was the first scheduled airline stop in Tennessee?

A. Chattanooga, on December 1, 1925, on the Atlanta-to-Evansville route.

Q. What two Federal programs helped boost Tennessee's aviation business in the 1920s and 1930s?

A. The Civil Works Administration (CWA) and the Works Progress Administration (WPA). (Berry Field in Nashville was one of the WPA's initial airport projects.)

Q. In post–Civil War Memphis, African Americans dominated the hack (taxi) and dray (freight) business until what two things put them out of business in the 1880s?

A. The influx of immigrants, which gave them competition, and the advent of the streetcar system.

Q. During World War II, Camp Tyson, near Paris, performed what unique function?

A. It was the nation's sole training center for operators of barrage balloons employed for aerial defense of the coasts.

Q. The administration of what governor, the first to die in office, created the Department of Highways and Public Works that paved many miles of roads?

A. Austin Peay.

Q. More than fifty wind-tunnels test the aerodynamics of everything from car engines to space rocket models at what center near Tullahoma?

A. Arnold Engineering Development Center, which performs tests to simulate flight conditions—even to speeds of Mach 20. The B-2 Spirit Stealth Bomber was researched and developed at the AEDC. (Next time you watch a space vehicle's well-timed re-entry, remember that the wind tunnel project helped bring it to earth safely.)

3

Before the War

Andrew Jackson and the Infamous Bell Witch

The quiet village of Adams in Robertson County, near the Kentucky line, is the site of such strange hauntings and supernatural occurrences that it's the only place of its kind to be designated with a Historical Marker by the state of Tennessee. Many people, curious about the so-called "Bell Witch," explore the now-famous Bell Witch Cave. Even future President Andrew Jackson couldn't resist investigating it for himself.

There are several stories about the origins of the Bell Witch. Some say it's the ghost of a neighbor, Kate Batts, who haunted farmer John Bell and his family. Others say it's an ancient Native American ghost—maybe several. What is known for certain is that the hauntings began around 1816, when John Bell and his family first became aware of a malevolent presence. The ghost threw heavy furniture, sang to visitors, quoted Scripture to visiting ministers, and pulled the hair of and otherwise tortured John Bell's daughters.

News of the hauntings spread, and people began coming from all over the county, then the state, and even other states, to see and hear the hauntings for themselves.

Then Andrew Jackson decided to come and rid the Bell family of their unwelcome visitor. The year was 1820, and the future seventh president was at his home, the Hermitage, in Nashville. John Bell Jr. had served Jackson in the military, and Jackson had a reputation for "braving the very harrows of Hell" to help a friend.

Gathering together a contingent of friends and servants, Jackson loaded a four-horse covered wagon as if he were on one of his military campaigns and

headed out. Toward the end of their journey, a strange thing happened. Nearing the Bell farm, one of Old Hickory's companions made "slighting remarks" about the Bell Witch. Just then, the wagon wheels froze, although the weather was fine and dry, and the wagon trail was firm and level. The driver whipped the horses, who only whinnied and reared in fright.

Checking the wagon himself and finding no reason for it to be stopped in its tracks, Jackson said, "It's the witch!" Then a voice came from nowhere: "All right, General, let the wagon move on. I'll see you tonight!" At that moment the wheels became free of their preternatural stays, and the party rolled on toward the Bell farm.

In 1820 Andrew Jackson traveled to the village of Adams to confront the infamous Bell Witch. (COURTESY TENNESSEE STATE MUSEUM; PAINTING BY AMANS; PHOTO BY JUNE DORMAN)

John Bell and his family welcomed the group; after supper, they all sat around the fireplace, telling stories and enjoying an after-dinner drink . . . or two. During this conversation, one of the men in the party began to brag that he was a "witch tamer" and had brought along a silver bullet for the sole purpose of killing the spirit. Just then they heard footsteps and a voice said, "All right, General, I am on hand, ready for business!"

The "witch tamer" was the one who caught the wrath of the spirit that night. He had imaginary "pins" stuck in his backside while the spirit taunted him to shoot. The spirit slapped the man's face repeatedly and finally had him running through the house and out the front door.

Finally "she" declared, "There's another fraud in your party, General. I'll get him tomorrow night." Jackson was eager to stay and see what else the Bell Witch would do, but the rest of his group was more than ready to return to Nashville the following morning. Jackson never again sought out the Bell Witch.

When asked about his adventure, he is reported to have remarked to his friends, "I saw nothing, but I heard enough to convince me that I would rather fight the British than deal with this torment they call the Bell Witch!"

Some years following this, John Bell died, haunted to his last days by a being who wouldn't let him rest. He and his family are buried in a cemetery near the house. Today, owners of the land say the area is still haunted, now with more than one being. It's still such a phenomenon that TV shows such as *Sightings* have come to investigate and have featured the Bell Cave in a documentary.

Whatever spooked the horses of Old Hickory's wagon and assaulted a member of his party is still there, wandering the grounds and the cave in Adams, Tennessee.

Did You Know? Tennessee's oldest community is not Chattanooga, Knoxville, Memphis, or even Nashville. While Jonesborough is Tennessee's oldest incorporated town, it's not Tennessee's oldest community. There are places that have been inhabited by Native Americans, but not continually. Formerly known as Trade Gap, tiny Trade, which lies between Mountain City, Tennessee, and Boone, North Carolina, claims the honor of being Tennessee's oldest community, with the longest continuous history of settlement. Trade is part of the old trail west, and this path was used by Creek, Yuchi, Shawnee, and Cherokee peoples. (Artifacts in the area are estimated to be at least one thousand years old.) Later, of course, pioneers such as Daniel Boone and early settlers traveled through and stopped to rest and exchange goods with the Indians in Trade. The area appears in maps made in 1749 by Peter Jefferson, Thomas Jefferson's father.

Town Names, Now and Then

Here are some Tennessee towns' original names, and their names as you know them today. See if you can match them up.

Now	Then
1. Jackson	A. Damascus
2. Clinton	B. Boat Yard
3. Bolivar	C. Burrville
4. Nashville	D. Alexandria
5. Bristol	E. Sapling Grove
6. Hartsville (east side)	F. Nashborough
7. Kingsport	G. Hatchie
8. Knoxville	H. White's Fort

Answers: 1. (D) 2. (C) 3. (G) 4. (F) 5. (E) 6. (A) 7. (B) 8. (H)

The Dogs Have Their Day at Fort Nashborough

The winter of 1781, as Tennessee winters go, was a hard one, with rain, snow, sleet, and bitter cold. The handful of settlers, who'd established Fort Nashborough two years earlier along the banks of the Cumberland River, were unprepared for such a hard season. The winter seemed interminable as their food and ammunition supplies dwindled.

At first their relationship with the local Cherokee people had been amicable, but they were on the western front in the Revolutionary War and both the British and the Spanish were encouraging the Indians to harass these newest settlers. The Cherokees began ambushing settlers who ventured out of the fort to hunt. Their horses and cows, which would determine the settlers' survival, were constantly being depleted by marauding bands of warriors. The fort's leader, Captain James Robertson, gave his followers hope with his unwavering bravery, but it was his wife's quick thinking that would ultimately save lives.

By April 1781, some settlers had been killed, others had died of disease, and others had simply left. Early one morning, some Cherokee warriors approached the fort, fired their guns, and left. It was a "cross this line" kind of tactic, and it worked. About twenty settlers went out after the Cherokee. Too late, the pioneers found themselves in an ambush. All around them were Indians firing upon them. Terrified of the gunfire, the settlers' horses reared, throwing their hapless riders, and bolted away.

Just then, the Captain's wife, Charlotte, known as "Mama Robertson," unleashed the fort dogs. There were about fifty of the fierce canines, who quickly came to their masters' aid. With bloodcurdling growls and snapping jaws, they leaped upon the warriors, allowing most of the settlers to hurry back to the protection of the fort. Some of the men who had been ambushed gave chase to the Cherokee warriors and defeated them in a skirmish near what is now Nickajack Dam.

There is a saying, "Every dog has his day." On that day in 1781, about fifty dogs had theirs, all at once.

The Story of "Beloved Woman"

Born in 1738, Nancy Ward, whose Cherokee name was Nanye-hi or "One Who Goes About," was first called "Beloved Woman" by her people because of her valor on the battlefield when she fought alongside her husband against the Creek. When her husband was killed in battle in 1755, she rallied the remaining warriors to victory. The Cherokee leaders often came to her for advice after this because they believed that the Great Spirit spoke through Beloved Woman.

She was friends with James Robertson and John Sevier and once saved Lydia Bean (wife of William Bean, the area's first recorded white settler in 1768) from being burned at the stake by Indians. She saved other settlers from Indian massacres as well, and from her friendship with white settlers, she learned of and introduced the Cherokee to dairy farming.

In helping to negotiate a treaty in July 1781 on the Long Island of the Holston River, Ward pleaded for peace on behalf of both white and Indian women. She also interceded in other treaty negotiations, again on behalf of the women and children on both sides. Because of this, she could be regarded as the first "feminist" in Tennessee.

Nancy Ward died in 1822; a monument at her grave site near Benton (near the Polk-McMinn County line) is a lasting tribute to the one the Cherokee called "Beloved Woman."

The Mystery of the Old Stone Fort

In Manchester, Old Stone Fort Archaeological State Park has what you might expect to find: campgrounds, hiking trails, picnic areas. But this has all been built around a "fort," which archaeologists say was built around A.D. 30, in the heyday of the Woodland Indians.

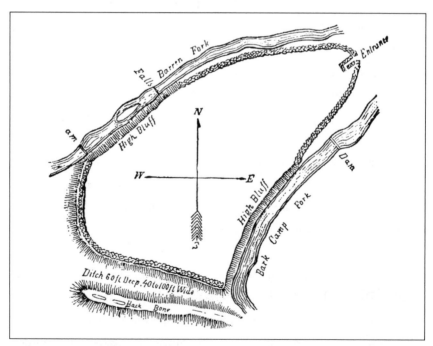

Construction on Old Stone Fort, a fifty-acre "hilltop enclosure" mound site in Manchester, was begun approximately two thousand years ago. Archaeologists are still uncertain of its original purpose. (COURTESY TENNESSEE DIVISION OF ARCHAEOLOGY)

According to Park Manager Ward Weems, the area was painstakingly built by many hands. He says construction on the site was begun approximately two thousand years ago and had most of its mound circumference in place before A.D. 200. The one-and-one-quarter-mile circumference of long mound walls and cliffs lying between the Big Duck and Little Duck Rivers set a limit or boundary to a special or ritual use area—not a controlling barrier, but a demarcating fence designating a special place.

Because few artifacts have been unearthed, it is believed that no one ever lived at this fifty-acre "hilltop enclosure" mound site. It was used as a purely ceremonial site. But for what types of ceremonies? No one knows for certain, although one hypothesis says it may have been used as a kind of celestial observatory.

One legend says that the Old Stone Fort is an ancient place of power and that spirits the Cherokee Indians called *sungnawyee eddahee,* or "night goers," wander here. Dr. Geoffrey Moorehead, a professor of mythology and legends at Salem University in Massachusetts, came to Manchester to investigate this spirit legend—and disappeared. Circumstances surrounding his fate remain a mystery.

Old Stone Fort harbors this and other enigmas. Experts have only been able to make educated guesses as to the religious practices of the Woodland Indians and their specific use for Old Stone Fort. The site is off the Manchester exit of I-24. It is accessible by foot and is surrounded by bluffs and rushing waters. Standing in the center of the flat meadow within the boundaries of the fort, maybe you'll feel a sense of mysticism yourself and gain some understanding of a place whose origins and purpose may forever remain unknown.

Other Interesting Archaeological Sites in Tennessee

★ **Fort Watauga:** Located in the Sycamore Shoals State Historical Area at Elizabethton is the site where, in 1772, the first American-born settlers formed a free and independent community called the Watauga Settlers Association.

★ **John and Landon Carter Mansion:** On the other side of Elizabethton is the oldest frame structure in Tennessee, built in 1780.

★ **Last Capital of the Cherokee:** In Red Clay lies the Cherokee's last capital before the forced march on the Trail of Tears.

★ **Pinson Mounds State Archaeological Area:** Just outside of Jackson is one of the largest Middle Woodland period archaeological sites in the Southeast.

★ **Chucalissa Village:** When the Civilian Conservation Corps (CCC) discovered this important Mississippian period archaeological site in Memphis in the 1930s, the *Memphis Press-Scimitar* reported the workers as being "ankle-deep in crumbling bones, bricks, and ancient pottery."

★ **Mound Bottom:** Near Dickson, associated with Montgomery Bell Park, is the largest Mississippian mound site in Tennessee.

★ **Frank H. McClung Museum:** On the University of Tennessee at Knoxville campus, this museum displays the Duck River Cache containing the largest collection of ceremonial flint-knapped items ever found in one cache in the United States.

"Lost" Counties of Tennessee

Two counties organized in Tennessee's earlier days later disappeared: Tennessee County, formed in 1788 in what is now Middle Tennessee, under the auspices of the state of North Carolina; and James County, created in 1871 in what is now southeastern Tennessee. Tennessee County was divided and pretty much absorbed by Robertson County in 1796; James was dissolved in 1890 to later became parts of Bradley and Hamilton Counties.

The Battle of Kings Mountain

During the American Revolution, men west of the Appalachian Mountains were, as one author put it, "just sitting out the War." Then in 1780 a British officer sent word to them, saying that if any of them *did* try to assist their rebellious eastern neighbors, he would "lay their country to waste with fire and sword." That did it. Inspired by a fiery sermon given by Reverend Samuel Doak, nine hundred "Overmountain Men" under Colonel William Campbell destroyed a force of eleven hundred Loyalists under Major Patrick Ferguson at the important battle of Kings Mountain in South Carolina.

TWO UNUSUAL MANSION TALES

The Love Story That Built a House

Historic Sites Director David Stieghan related to me the tale of how Rippavilla Plantation in Spring Hill was built because of a love story. It began with a man named Nathaniel Cheairs, who had ten children, the youngest one named after the father. In 1841 the younger Nathaniel fell in love with a girl named Susan McKissack and wanted to marry her, but his father was against it. One day the father and son had "the talk." It went something like this:

"Why don't you want me to marry Susan? What's wrong with her?"

"Nothing's wrong with her; it's just her name."

"Her name?"

"Yes, son. You see, I married a girl named Sarah, just as my father did, and his father before him, and his father before him, and his father before *him*." The elder Nathaniel looked at his son. "Can't you find a Sarah who'll do just as well?"

The young man thought for a minute. "No, father. I love Susan."

Every single brick in Rippavilla mansion was made in William McKissack's kiln as a wedding present to his daughter. (COURTESY RIPPAVILLA PLANTATION)

There was a dramatic pause, then, "Son, I'll give you five thousand dollars in gold if you agree not to marry Susan. It'll be breaking a family tradition."

The son was again silent for a moment. "Father, Susan's father is William McKissack and he owns a brick kiln. He's one of the richest men in the county, and his slaves are skilled brick masons and carpenters. Surely, she'll bring more than five thousand dollars into this marriage."

The younger Nathaniel had his way. He married his Susan, and ten years later they started building Rippavilla mansion. Susan's father gave them something special as a wedding present: every single brick in the mansion, which still stands in Spring Hill, was made in the McKissack kiln as a wedding present to the young couple.

Incidentally, young Nathaniel wasn't disowned by his father. On the contrary, upon his father's death the youngest child in the family got the lion's share of the estate, including the fifteen-hundred-acre plantation!

Rattle and Snap: A Gambler's Tale (or, Your Tax Dollars at Work!)

It was 1792 and Tennessee was still part of North Carolina. William Polk, a Revolutionary War hero, and his friend Alexander Martin, the governor of North Carolina, were involved in a gambling game played with dice (though some say dried beans). Legend has it they were sitting in the halls of the North Carolina legislature.

Martin had recently come into nearly six thousand acres of land from General Nathanael Greene, who had fallen on hard times. He had paid the taxes on the land in what is now Maury County and had taken title to it. When the betting got heavy, Martin put up his land, and with a fateful roll of the dice (or a throw of the beans), William Polk won it.

One of Polk's sons built a house on the land and named it after the game, Rattle and Snap. The present owner, Amon Evans, former publisher of the *Tennessean* in Nashville, says most architectural scholars herald Rattle and Snap as one of the two finest examples of Greek Revival architecture in the country. Situated in Columbia, it is open to the public.

Historic Homes and Sites You Can Visit

This list, provided by the Tennessee Historical Commission, is divided into the three "Grand Divisions" of the state. Not all of the sites were built before the war.

★   <u>West Tennessee</u>
   Alex Haley House Museum (Henning)
   Ames Plantation (Grand Junction)
   Arlington Historic Post Office
   The Buford Pusser Home and Museum (near Savannah)
   Casey Jones Home and Railroad Museum (Jackson)
   Chucalissa Archaeological Museum (Memphis)
   Church Park (Memphis)
   Collierville Town Square and Railroad Cars
   David Crockett Cabin (Morristown)
   Davies Manor (Brunswick)
   Elmwood Cemetery (Memphis)
   Fort Pillow State Historic Area (near Garland)
   Freed House (Memphis)
   Gotten House (north of Memphis)

Hannum-Rhea House (Somerville)

The Little Courthouse Museum (Bolivar)

Magevney House (Memphis)

Mallory-Neely House (Memphis)

The Pillars (Bolivar)

Pinson Mounds State Archaeological Area (near Jackson)

Reelfoot Lake Resort Park (Tiptonville)

Shiloh National Military Park

Woodruff-Fontaine House (Memphis)

★ Middle Tennessee

The Athenaeum (Columbia)

Belle Meade Plantation (Nashville)

Belmont Mansion (Nashville)

Bowen Plantation House (Nashville)

Carnton Plantation (Franklin)

Carter House (Franklin)

Cookeville Depot Museum

Cordell Hull Birthplace and Museum (near Byrdstown)

Cragfont (near Gallatin)

Cravens House (Chattanooga)

Fort Donelson National Battlefield (Dover)

Fort Nashborough (Nashville)

The Hermitage (Nashville)

Hohenwald Depot

The Homeplace 1850 (near Dover)

James K. Polk Home (Columbia)

Natchez Trace Parkway and Meriwether Lewis Monument (near Hohenwald)

Oaklands Historic House Museum (Murfreesboro)

The Parthenon (Nashville)

Rock Castle (near Hendersonville)

Sam Davis Home (near Smyrna)

Sergeant York Home (Jamestown)

Smith-Trahern Mansion (Clarksville)

Sparta Rock House

Stones River National Battlefield (near Murfreesboro)

Tennessee State Capitol (Nashville)

Travellers Rest (Nashville)

Trousdale Place (Hartsville)

Tulip Grove (between Nashville and Lebanon)

Wynnewood (outside Gallatin)

★ <u>East Tennessee</u>

Andrew Johnson National Historic Site (Greeneville)

Armstrong-Lockett House (Crescent Bend)

Beck Cultural Exchange Center (Knoxville)

Blount Mansion (Knoxville)

Burra Burra Mine Site (Ducktown)

Cades Cove (near Gatlinburg)

Davy Crockett Birthplace State Park (near Jonesborough)

Etowah L&N Depot

The Exchange Place (Kingsport)

Fort Loudon State Historic Area (near Madisonville)

James White Fort (outside Knoxville)

Mabry-Hazen House (Knoxville)

Marble Springs (near Sevierville)

The Netherland Inn (Kingsport)

Old Roane County Courthouse (near Lenoir City)

President Andrew Johnson Museum Library (near Greeneville)

Ramsey House (Knoxville)

Red Clay State Historic Park (Cleveland)

Rhea County Courthouse and Scopes Trial Museum (Dayton)

Rocky Mount (Elizabethton)

Rugby

Sam Houston Schoolhouse (Maryville)

Samuel Doak House (Greeneville)

Tipton-Haynes Historic Site (Johnson City)

BEFORE THE WAR TRIVIA

Q. What county is known as the Antebellum Homes Capital of Tennessee?

A. Maury. Among its many antebellum homes are the four Polk family homes: the James K. Polk Ancestral Home, Hamilton Place (Lucius Polk's Palladian manor), St. John's at Ashwood, and Rattle and Snap.

Q. When it was governed by William Blount, what was Tennessee's original name before statehood?

A. The Territory of the United States South of the River Ohio.

Q. By defeating what Indian nation at the battle of Horseshoe Bend in 1814 did Andrew Jackson add twenty-three million acres of land in present-day Georgia and Alabama to the United States?

A. Creek.

Q. Land now occupied by Jackson, Tennessee, was acquired from what Native American tribe?

A. Chickasaw.

Q. What pioneer was hired to head a group of woodsmen to improve and connect existing Indian trails to form the famous Wilderness Road through the Cumberland Gap to help the westward expansion of the American nation?

A. Daniel Boone.

Q. What invention made cities on the water such as Memphis and Nashville major trading centers in the nineteenth century?

A. The steamboat.

Q. The first of several such groups, the Cumberland Agricultural Society was formed in 1819 in what county to help farmers improve farming techniques?

A. Davidson.

Q. To aid him in his fight against the British during the battle of New Orleans, Andrew Jackson allied himself with what Louisiana-based pirate?

A. Jean Laffite.

Q. According to census records, when the Civil War began, what percentage of the population of Tennessee was slaves?

A. Around 25 percent (283,019 people).

Q. What small town in West Tennessee has more than one hundred buildings on the National Register of Historic Places?

A. Bolivar.

Q. What is the total area of the state of Tennessee?

A. 42,144 square miles, including 989 square miles of inland water.

Q. On what day did Congress approve admission of Tennessee as the sixteenth state?

A. June 1, 1796.

Q. The name *Tennessee* comes from what Indian word?

A. *Tanasi,* a Yuchi word meaning "old town"; the Native Americans used this word for a village and gave the same name to the Little Tennessee and Tennessee Rivers.

Q. How many ships were constructed at the navy yard in Memphis between 1844 and 1857?

A. One, the USS *Allegheny.*

Q. In 1540 what Spaniard led the first European expedition into Tennessee territory?

A. Hernando de Soto.

Q. What five major Indian tribes originally inhabited the Tennessee region?

A. Cherokee, Chickasaw, Creek, Chickamauga, and Choctaw.

Q. In 1819 what three Tennesseans bought five thousand acres from the

U.S. government and organized a settlement on the Mississippi River which they named Memphis?

A. General Andrew Jackson, Judge John Overton, and General James Winchester.

Q. What Tennessee county was named after a Revolutionary War hero and the first governor of Kentucky?

A. Shelby, whose county seat is Memphis, after Isaac Shelby.

Q. What Scottish lady and visionary heiress founded the short-lived utopian colony near Nashoba in 1827?

A. Frances Wright.

Q. An unsuccessful plan to create a canal between the Hatchie and Tennessee Rivers was attempted by what colorful early Tennessean?

A. David Crockett.

Q. In 1835 Newton Cannon became what party's first governor of Tennessee?

A. Whig.

Q. What four Tennessee towns have served as the state capital?

A. Knoxville, Kingston (for one day), Murfreesboro, and Nashville.

Q. Why was Kingston the state capital for only one day, September 21, 1807?

A. To satisfy a treaty requirement with the Cherokee.

Q. What gunboat fired the first shot of the Spanish-American War?

A. USS *Nashville*.

Q. Captain William Atkinson mustered fifty-seven volunteers from what county for the war against Mexico?

A. Hamblen. (Because so many Tennesseans volunteered to fight in the Mexican War, Tennessee became known as "the Volunteer State.")

Q. What small Indian boy, orphaned during the Creek War, did Andrew Jackson bring home to raise as his own?

A. Lincoya.

4

Famous Tennesseans

The Story of Casey Jones

Jonathan Luther "Casey" Jones was an engineer for the Illinois Central rail line when he had his fateful crash the night of April 29, 1900. More than two hundred songs have been written and published about him and his tragic end.

A substitute for the regular engineer for this route, Jones had taken out Engine Number 382, the Cannonball, when he realized that the switch at Vaughan, Mississippi, was blocked. Knowing his train would crash into the oncoming train, he stayed at the

On display at Casey Jones Village in Jackson are a portrait of "the brave engineer," the pocket watch Jones carried the night of his death, and an artist's rendering of the famous train wreck. (Courtesy Casey Jones Village)

controls to apply the hand brake, telling the fireman to jump to safety. All the passengers survived the crash; Casey Jones was the single fatality.

The first person to compose verses about Jones's self-sacrifice was Wallace Saunders, a black engine-wiper and friend of Casey. He wrote the original song, "Casey Jones, the Brave Engineer." Jones has been immortalized in hundreds of songs, in literature, and with a museum in his honor in Jackson, Tennessee, where he made his home.

Casey Jones, the Brave Engineer

Come all you rounders if you want to hear
A story about a brave Engineer.
Casey Jones was the Rounder's name,
On a six eight-wheeler, boys, he won his fame.
The caller called Casey at half-past four.
He kissed his wife at the station door.
He mounted to the Cabin with his orders in his hand
And he took his farewell trip to that Promised Land.

(Chorus)
Casey Jones, mounted to the cabin,
Casey Jones, with his orders in his hand,
Casey Jones, mounted to the cabin,
And he took his farewell trip to the Promised Land.

"Put in your water and shovel in your coal,
Put your head out the window, watch them drivers roll.
I'll run her till she leaves the rail
'Cause I'm eight hours late with that western mail."
He looked at his watch and his watch was slow,
He looked at the water and the water was low,
He turned to the Fireman and then he said,
"We're goin' to reach Canton but we'll all be dead."

(Chorus)
Casey Jones, going to reach Canton,
Casey Jones, but we'll all be dead,
Casey Jones, going to reach Canton,
"We're going to reach Canton, but we'll all be dead."

Casey pulled up that Southern Hill.
He tooted for the crossing with an awful shrill.
The switchmen know by the engine's moan
That the man at the throttle was Casey Jones.
He pulled up within two miles of the place.
Number One stared him right in the face.
He turned to the Fireman and said, "Sir, you'd better jump,
'Cause there's two locomotives that's a-goin' to bump."

(Chorus)
Casey Jones, two locomotives,
Casey Jones, that's a-goin' to bump,
Casey Jones, two locomotives,
"There's two locomotives that's a-goin' to bump."

Headaches and heartaches and all kinds of pain
Are not apart from a railroad train
Tales that are earnest, noble and grand
Belong to the life of a railroad man.
Mrs. Jones sat on her bed a-sighin',
Just received a message that Casey was dying.
Said, "Go to bed, children, and hush your crying
'Cause your Daddy's now ridin' on that heavenly line."

(Chorus)
Casey Jones, mounted to the cabin,

Casey Jones, with his orders in his hand,

Casey Jones, mounted to the cabin,

And he took his farewell trip to the Promised Land.

(Courtesy of the Casey Jones Home and Railroad Museum)

The "Unsinkable" Kathy Bates

Born Kathleen Doyle Bates in Memphis in 1948, this woman who played the role of Margaret "Molly" Brown in James Cameron's blockbuster movie *Titanic* almost didn't take the part. She'd already committed to doing two other movies, but then one fell through and rehearsals for the other clashed with Bates's schedule.

She admits she was "made" for the role: "If you ever see a picture of Molly Brown, I look just like her," she told a *Washington Post* interviewer during shooting for the film.

This "unsinkable" Tennessean keeps a frenetic pace: after all the grueling work required to make *Titanic,* her schedule kept her from attending the movie's premiere. Bates went later, with some friends, and bought her own ticket. And unlike many enthusiastic *Titanic* fans, that was the only time she saw it in a theater.

"Steamboatin' Tom" Ryman: Not Your Everyday Romantic Type

You probably know the Ryman Auditorium, the long-time home of the Grand Ole Opry, was built by Tom Ryman as a religious tabernacle after his conversion. Nashville-born Ryman, known as "Steamboatin' Tom," was probably the most successful steamboating man plying the waters of the Cumberland, Tennessee, and Ohio Rivers beginning in the 1870s.

Before steamboats were commonly used, the only way for riverside-dwelling farmers to get their produce and livestock to market was by hand-hewn raft—it was a long and dangerous trip downstream and impossible to go upstream. Entrepreneur Ryman finally saved the three thousand dollars he needed to buy his first steamboat, and made the trip to New Orleans to fetch it. He found his boat—already named, appropriately enough, the *Alpha*—and piloted her home himself.

A year later, he married Mary Elizabeth Baugh of Franklin, and the wedding was attended by some of the best-known riverboat captains on the river. The week-long "wedding cruise" from Nashville to Evansville, Indiana, was aboard the *Alpha*—with thirty-five guests on board.

It was on the return voyage, when they were off the Ohio River and back on the Cumberland, that Steamboatin' Tom had all his honeymoon dreams realized. He was in a race against another steamboat, the *Tyrone*, and Steamboatin' Tom came close to losing it until he harangued his engineer and workmen to accelerate to the highest possible speed. The *Alpha* overtook and passed the *Tyrone*, as the honeymoon party cheered and waved their handkerchiefs at the defeated crew.

Such was the honeymoon trip of Steamboatin' Tom Ryman.

Jack Daniel and George Dickel

The areas around Lynchburg and Tullahoma are lovely, with rolling hills, natural limestone springs, iron-free water, and fertile soil. Agricultural types might look at this and think "corn" or "cattle." Jasper Newton "Jack" Daniel and George Dickel thought "whiskey."

Jack Daniel's career in the distillery business began in 1860 at the tender age of twelve, when he worked with Dan Call near Lynchburg. By 1863, Daniel was Call's partner; three years later, he bought out Call's interest. The teenaged Daniel was a distillery owner, but by today's laws was still too young to drink what he produced.

Also in the late 1860s, Tullahoma resident George A. Dickel became a partner in the whiskey-making business with two Nashville families, the Schwabs and Davises. They got their whiskey from several regional sources, and the most favored was out of Cascade Creek in Coffee County. Eventually Dickel created his own blend made especially for the tastes of his fans in Nashville. When he died in 1894, his wife, Augusta, managed the business with his partners.

In 1910, when prohibition became law in Tennessee, both distilleries moved—Jack Daniel's to St. Louis (after Daniel's death when his nephew Lem Motlow had taken over the business), and George Dickel's to Louisville. When the national Prohibition Amendment was repealed in 1933, they moved back to their original counties. Although their home counties were both "dry," they finally relented and voted (by narrow margins) to allow the distilleries to come back and once again make whiskey.

Alvin York, Education's Agent

You know Alvin York was the most decorated soldier of World War I. What you may not know is what York did for education in Tennessee after he came home.

Alvin York, the most decorated soldier of World War I, was drafted despite his stance as a conscientious objector. He later established the York Institute in Fentress County.
(COURTESY TENNESSEE STATE MUSEUM PHOTOGRAPHIC ARCHIVES)

Born in 1887 in Pall Mall, Tennessee, York was one of eleven children whose father was a subsistence farmer. In his early days York enjoyed shooting his gun and fighting, and he had little education and few skills. Some said then he'd never amount to much.

In 1914 he was, as southerners say, "born again," when he went to a revival of the Church of Christ in Christian Union, a small religious sect with followers in Tennessee, Ohio, and Kentucky. While attending church there, he met his future wife, Gracie Williams.

York's church held convictions against violence, war in particular, so when he received his draft card, he scrawled on it, "Dont [sic] want to fight." His stand as a conscientious objector was short-lived, however. The local and state review boards denied him that status because his church was not recognized as a "legitimate Christian sect."

Once York became a soldier, his company commander had several talks with him and convinced the young man war could be morally right when it was necessary to fight. The rest, as they say, is history. In a skirmish in October 1918, with only the aid of a few men, York silenced the enemy's machine guns, capturing 132 prisoners. He was a national hero but still felt dissatisfied. He'd never felt comfortable with his lack of education, so upon his return home he worked to establish a school in Fentress County. He was so dedicated to his vision that in the lean years he even paid teachers' salaries and purchased buses. Today the York Institute is one of the largest high school campuses in the world—more than fourteen thousand acres.

Pass Me My Horse, Too, Please

One of the earliest white settlers in Middle Tennessee, Thomas Sharp Spencer had strength the stuff of which legends are made. Breaking up a fight once, he threw a militiaman over a rail fence. The soldier apparently recovered quickly enough to make a request of Spencer, saying something like this: "Would you throw my horse over, too, so I can leave?"

Luke Lea: Soldier, Newspaperman, Senator—and Kidnapper?

It was New Year's Day 1919. The Armistice had been signed two months before, and while waiting to be shipped back home, Colonel Luke Lea, commander of the 114th Field Artillery (National Guard) Unit, brooded in Luxembourg. He was dissatisfied because the person responsible for the destruction and misery caused by the war, the German kaiser, had been granted asylum and was currently living in the castle of Count Bentinck in Holland. Lea thought the kaiser should go to Paris to be tried for war crimes, instead of allowing his people to suffer severe war reparations for his deeds.

Therefore, Lea decided if the kaiser wouldn't go of his own volition, then

Dissatisfied with the course of justice at the end of World War I, Colonel Luke Lea attempted to kidnap the German kaiser to bring him to trial for his war crimes. (COURTESY TENNESSEE STATE MUSEUM PHOTOGRAPHIC ARCHIVES)

Lea would see that he went. Lea rounded up a handful of his fellow Tennesseans, telling them they were going on a secret mission. He got passes for them, and they headed out that same day. Their mission: kidnap the kaiser and bring him to justice!

Lea was accustomed to getting his own way. Founder of the Nashville *Tennessean*, former U.S. senator, and forceful in his opinions, he didn't let a washed-out bridge on the Rhine or being stopped at two borders deter him from his mission. The group bluffed its way past everyone who stopped them, saying they were on official business for their country.

Once inside the castle and face to face with Count Bentinck, Lea repeatedly requested an audience with the kaiser; it was just as many times denied. With no kaiser forthcoming and German soldiers all around the chateau, Lea abandoned his mission. He and his men returned to Luxembourg and from there, home to the United States.

Lea received an "official" reprimand from his commander in chief, General Pershing. After the incident, Pershing was reported to have said, "I'd have given a year's pay to have been able to take Lea's trip into Holland, and to have entered the castle of Count Bentinck without invitation."

Ernest P. Worrell: "Know What I Mean, Vern?"

Now you know this man who played up his "red-neckness" as the guy with the bill cap who did commercials for a variety of products all over the country. In many of these he addressed his unseen friend, "Vern," and the commercials became so popular that Tennesseans took to using his expression, "Know what I mean, Vern?" in conversations when they wanted to make sure they were understood.

Although he died February 11, 2000, Ernest P. Worrell (a.k.a. Jim Varney) has left us a treasure trove of belly-laughing films. They include *Ernest: Scared Stupid* (1992), *Ernest Saves Christmas* (1989), *Ernest Goes to Camp* (1987), *Ernest Goes to Jail* (1990), *Ernest Goes to School* (1994), *Ernest in the Army* (1998), *Ernest Rides Again* (1994), and *Slam Dunk Ernest* (1995), in which he shared the spotlight with Kareem Abdul-Jabar.

This just goes to show what any Tennessean with feistiness, a pleasantly skewed sense of humor, and a bill cap can do.

Know what I mean?

Guess Who? These two African American civil rights activists helped found the National Association for the Advancement of Colored People (NAACP). She got her start in journalism after being forcibly removed from a first-class ladies' coach in Memphis because of her color, after which she wrote of that experience under the pen name Iola. He was a graduate of Fisk University in Nashville who joined forces with her in an effort to increase racial equality and protest violence against African Americans, especially lynchings. They began the National Negro Conference, which grew into the NAACP.

Who are they? Ida B. Wells-Barnett and W. E. B. DuBois.

Dolly Parton, the Creative Dreamer of East Tennessee

As a student growing up in sight of the Pigeon River in East Tennessee, Dolly Parton was assigned to give a book report to the class. She was an avid reader, so this was no problem. But Dolly was a dreamer, too, with a mischievous spark in her, and she loved to make things up. She rose to the challenge of the book report. When the time came for her to give her report, she stood up and fabricated the entire "book," including a fictitious author's name, title of the book, and subject matter.

Today Dolly Parton is a successful singer, actress, and the owner of

Dollywood and other attractions in Pigeon Forge. When she recalled those school days, she admitted she's sure her teacher realized her fabrication, but never said a thing about it. She went on to write stories and songs, but when it came time for her to write her autobiography, "that was the hardest thing," she stated in her book *My Life and Other Unfinished Business.* "I had to tell the truth."

Dolly Parton's creative dreaming allowed her to come up from incredibly poor beginnings and make her dreams realities.

Did You Know? Dolly Parton's Dollywood in Pigeon Forge is the number one tourist attraction in Tennessee.

Martha Ingram: The "Cultured" Pearl of Music City

All good mothers try to offer the best for their children. In Nashville, one mother not only created a cultural environment for her children, but was instrumental in making Nashville into a cultural Mecca.

This woman with the effervescent smile and down-to-earth personality was born Martha Robinson Rivers in Charleston, South Carolina. Although she had a good childhood, it was when she went to Vassar that she was really exposed to the performing arts. In New York City on a blind date she met Erskine Bronson Ingram. This was one blind date that went well, for they married and had four children. They moved to Nashville, where Martha Ingram wanted her children to have the same love of the fine arts that she had. The only way to do this was to create that environment herself. She became determined to make Music City a more cultured city.

In 1973 she and a handful of other dedicated philanthropists were able to build the Tennessee Performing Arts Center (TPAC). That was only the beginning of what she was to do.

When her husband died in 1995, he was Tennessee's only billionaire. His business, Ingram Industries, was ranked by *Forbes* magazine as number 14 of the top 500 privately held corporations in the United States. Ingram Industries, of which Martha Ingram is now CEO, includes a barge transportation business, a large book distribution company, a software distribution company, and an insurance company.

With intellect, enthusiasm, and commitment, Ingram continued to turn her good fortune toward a higher purpose. In April 1998, this woman whom *Forbes* named the wealthiest businesswoman in the country, kicked off a fundraising campaign she called "Symphony 2000." Its main goal was to fund an endowment to elevate the Nashville Symphony to a level of national prominence.

Martha Ingram, the CEO of Ingram Industries, has devoted herself to bringing the fine arts to Music City. (COURTESY MARTHA INGRAM)

Next time you attend a ballet, an opera, or a symphony performance in Nashville, send a mental note of thanks to the Pearl of Music City, Martha Ingram.

Walking Tall: Buford Pusser

Born in Adamsville in 1937, Buford Pusser went to high school in Oklahoma, then joined the marines but took a medical discharge because of an asthmatic condition. Back in Adamsville, he became a semipro wrestler and met his future wife, Pauline Mullins. They married in 1959 and moved to Chicago, where he worked as a die-cutter, until destiny called for his return to Adamsville.

There he finally found his calling. Incensed over the locally rampant illicit whiskey trade, Pusser ran against the incumbent constable and won in an upset victory by more than one hundred votes. Then he ran against the McNairy County sheriff, James Dickey, who was involved with a moonshine ring operating illegally at the borders of the Tennessee and Mississippi state lines. Dickey was a dyed-in-the-wool Democrat in a county of the same leanings; Pusser was a Republican. When Dickey was killed in an automobile accident before election day, Pusser's position as sheriff was assured.

The members of the moonshine ring came after Pusser. Ambushes against him began in November 1964. Despite being stabbed seven times, shot eight times, and run over by a car, Pusser persisted in his war on the illegal whiskey trade. The first year on the job, he arrested seventy-five moonshiners and raided forty-two stills. In later years, he took on illegal gambling houses and prostitution rings. When his wife was killed in a 1967 ambush meant for him, Pusser became even more determined to root out the criminals.

In 1969 he was recognized for his one-man anticrime crusade by the Tennessee General Assembly, which made him an honorary sergeant of arms. His sheriffing days ended in 1970, but three movies were made of his life. The first one, *Walking Tall,* was a box-office success in 1973, and millions of Americans came to know Pusser as the no-nonsense sheriff who meant business. Unfortunately, Pusser would never get to see the other two films of his life (*Walking Tall II* in 1976 and *Walking Tall III: The Final Chapter* in 1977). He died in a car wreck in 1974.

A Tennessee Senator with Hollywood Credits

As of May 2000, Senator Fred Thompson of Tennessee had amassed twenty-seven professional acting credits—eighteen films, six made-for TV movies, and four appearances on television series.

★ Films

 Marie (1985), with Sissy Spacek

 No Way Out (1987), with Kevin Costner and Gene Hackman

 Feds (1988), with Rebecca DeMornay

 Fat Man and Little Boy (1989), with Paul Newman

 Hunt for Red October (1990), with Sean Connery

 Die Hard II (1990), with Bruce Willis

Days of Thunder (1990), with Tom Cruise

Flight of the Intruder (1990), with Danny Glover and Willem Dafoe

Class Action (1991), with Gene Hackman

Necessary Roughness (1991), with Scott Bakula

Curly Sue (1991), with Jim Belushi

Cape Fear (1991), with Robert DeNiro

Thunderheart (1992), with Val Kilmer

White Sands (1992), with Mickey Rourke and Willem Dafoe

Aces: Iron Eagle III (1992), with Lou Gossett Jr.

Born Yesterday (1993), with Melanie Griffith and Don Johnson

In the Line of Fire (1993), with Clint Eastwood

Baby's Day Out (1994), with Joe Mantegna

★ Television Movies

Unholy Matrimony (1988), with Patrick Duffy

Bed of Light (1992), with Susan Dey

Stay the Night (1992), with Jane Alexander

Keep the Change (1992), with William Peterson

Dayo (1992), with Delta Burke

Barbarians at the Gate (1993), with James Garner

★ Television Series

Matlock (1986)

Wiseguy (1987)

China Beach (1988)

Roseanne (1988)

The Audition That Gave Her the Name

Frances Rose Shore sat waiting in the studio of radio station WNEW in New York City. She had sold everything she owned to come to the city to make it as a singer. This, her first audition, had to be the best performance of her young life. As she waited for her name to be called, she thought about what she really wanted for a stage name. Nothing came immediately to mind.

Born in 1917 in Winchester, Tennessee, Fannie Rose was accustomed to fighting against odds. Stricken with polio when she was eighteen months old, she was left with a crippled leg, requiring her to relearn how to walk. If it hadn't been for her mother, who pushed her to keep exercising in such sports as tennis, Fannie Rose might never have recovered as fully as she did.

Dinah Shore hosts Nancy Reagan on her TNN talk show. (COURTESY THE *HERALD CHRONICLE,* WINCHESTER, TENN.)

The family moved to Nashville where Fannie Rose went to Hume Fogg High School and was active in theatricals. Her biggest obstacle in her dream to be a professional singer was her father. When he found out she was really serious about a singing career, he cut off her charge accounts and her allowance. By keeping her broke, her dad thought he could keep Fannie Rose at home.

The determined young girl got a job singing on a local radio station and finished college at Vanderbilt University; then she sold everything she owned to raise funds to go to New York.

Finally it came time for her to audition and she was told to sing the song "Dinah." She was hired and the folks at the studio began calling her "Dinah," the name she adopted. Multitalented Dinah Shore went on to enjoy fabulous success as a recording artist; a radio, TV, and movie entertainer; and a cookbook author.

She was a star of the first magnitude—spunky, cheerful, with a wide trademark smile, and a kiss to the audience at the end of every TV show. Dinah Shore continued to perform until she died in 1994. In her hometown of Winchester, the townspeople honored her by calling a boulevard by the name she chose after her audition: Dinah Shore.

Patricia Neal: Because of a Fly . . .

You may know that Patricia Neal was born in Kentucky in 1926 but was raised in Knoxville, where she began to develop her career in the performing arts. You may know she performed in Lillian Hellman's drama *The Little Foxes*, then signed a contract with Warner Brothers in 1947. You may recall her roles in *The Fountainhead* and *The Hasty Heart,* her ill-fated romance with Gary Cooper, or her doomed marriage to author Roald Dahl. You may remember she was Tennessee's Woman of the Year in 1962 and that she starred in Tennessee Williams's play *Cat on a Hot Tin Roof* and in the Broadway production of *The Miracle Worker.*

But you may not know about the strange thing that happened on the set of the 1963 movie *Hud,* which led Neal to give her most "natural" performance. The director had yelled, "All quiet on the set!" and "Action!" Then something happened that wasn't in the script. "I was standing on the front porch and I was making cheese," Neal recalled, "and Paul [Newman] was about to come in. Just then, a fly came on the screen of the window, and instinctively I slapped at it with my towel. I was just acting normally. We continued on with the scene, and the director decided to keep on filming." She paused and quipped, "I don't think flies take direction, do you?"

After the director viewed the footage, the "fly scene" remained in the movie; in 1963 Neal won the Academy Award for best actress for her role in *Hud.* "The fly won it for me," she said.

The fly was unavailable for comment.

Samuel Jackson

Samuel Leroy Jackson was born in Washington, D.C., in 1948, but was raised in Chattanooga. He's a successful actor now, but an incident during his college years nearly put an end to his promising beginnings.

It happened in 1969, when Jackson was a junior at Atlanta's Morehouse College. He and other students were protesting the skewed ratio of black-to-white trustees at the predominantly African American college and were demanding a curriculum of African American studies. Trying to force the issue and gain media attention, Jackson and his friends took members of the college's board of trustees hostage and locked them in a building on campus. One of those taken was Martin Luther King Sr., father of the slain civil rights leader.

Jackson and his comrades held the hostages for two days. When it was over, he and the other students responsible for the incident were expelled but were later reinstated.

Despite such shaky academic beginnings, Jackson graduated in 1972 with a degree in theater arts. Later, Jackson's big break came when he played Gator in *Jungle Fever* (1991), which won him the New York Film Critics Circle Award for best supporting actor and was also acclaimed at the Cannes Film Festival. Since that time he's been in more than twenty films; he's probably best known for the character Jules, the hit man in Quentin Tarantino's *Pulp Fiction* (1994), for which he got an Academy Award for best supporting actor. Incidentally, Tarantino is a Tennessee native.

More Claims to Fame

Here is a short list of other actors and actresses from Tennessee:

★ **Cybill Shepherd:** Named after her grandfather (Cy) and her father (Bill), Cybill Shepherd won a Golden Globe Award for best actress in the TV sit-com *Cybill* and maintains a home in Memphis.

★ **Cherry Jones:** A native of Paris, Tennessee, Cherry Jones starred in the 1999 made-for-TV movie *Murder in a Small Town*. She also starred as Liz Hammond (opposite Robert Redford) in the 1998 movie *The Horse Whisperer*.

★ **Dixie Carter:** Born in McLemoresville and a graduate of Memphis's Rhodes College, this soft-spoken epitome of traditional Tennessee womanhood is known for the sit-com *Designing Women* and for commercials advertising General Foods' International Coffees and the Yellow Pages.

★ **Morgan Freeman:** Memphis-born Morgan Freeman almost quit acting out of frustration and considered becoming a taxi driver instead.
Ironically, his most famous role was that of Hoke Colburn, the
chauffeur for Jessica Tandy's character in the hit movie *Driving Miss
Daisy*, for which he received an Oscar nomination.

Oh, to What Heights They Will Go!

You may know that Tennessee's highest mountain is named for the
mountain climber and U.S. senator Thomas Lanier Clingman, but there's an
unusual story about how Clingman's Dome got its name. It started with a
dispute between Clingman and a University of North Carolina professor,
Elisha Mitchell, as to what peak in the Appalachian Mountains was the highest. Mitchell claimed Black Dome in North Carolina and Clingman said it
was Tennessee's Smoky Dome.

While doing altitude checks of Black Dome, Mitchell accidentally
drowned in a stream. Clingman then hired Arnold Guyot, a Swiss-born
geographer, to make a study of the mountains. At 6,643 feet, Smoky Dome
(now Clingman's Dome) is the highest point in Tennessee, but Black Dome
(now Mount Mitchell) won the debate, at 6,684 feet.

Did You Know? This Mississippi-born girl once approached
a famous singer as she was stepping from her limousine and told her she
had no money and was without a place to stay. The singer gave her one
hundred dollars and the girl used it for hotel accommodations.

The girl? Oprah Winfrey, who came to live in Nashville when she was
thirteen. She later attended Tennessee State University and was a news
reporter for radio station WVOL and the CBS television station in
Nashville. The Chicago-based *Oprah Winfrey Show* is America's top-rated
talk show today. Oh—and the singer who helped her? Memphis-born
Aretha Franklin.

Inner Vision

Francis Joseph Campbell was born in Franklin County in 1832 and attended school in Nashville. He was a quick learner, became a teacher, was cofounder of a college in England, and was knighted by King Edward VII in 1909. He also became something of a mountain climber, and even ascended Mount Blanc in the Alps.

None of this is especially noteworthy until you know the rest of the story. For Francis Campbell had been blind since the age of four and is the only blind person ever to climb Mount Blanc. The school he cofounded was the Royal College for the Blind in London.

The First Man-Made Tunnel in the United States

Tennessee's first capitalist and industrialist, Montgomery Bell, came from Pennsylvania's iron-producing country and in 1804 purchased Cumberland Furnace from "the Father of Tennessee," James Robertson. This was the beginning of his empire. Bell then bought some land located on the Narrows of the Harpeth River, so called because it flows within a couple of hundred feet of itself, twisting around the base of a bluff. Bell became inspired by what the power of water could do for a furnace, and he had his slaves work for three years, boring a three-hundred-foot-long, fifteen-foot-wide tunnel through the base of the bluff. This diverted some of the water to flow through the tunnel, and the seventeen-foot drop on the other side turned wheels to provide power for Bell's furnace, which he called Pattison Forge or (Petterson Forge), after his mother.

Bell's tunnel is believed to be the first man-made tunnel in the United States, and his forge provided the cannon balls used by Andrew Jackson's men in the battle of New Orleans.

An Accident Leads to an Invention

A boy named George was born in eastern Tennessee around 1760. His mother was Wurtah, daughter of a prominent Cherokee family, and his father was Nathaniel Gist (or Guess), a fur trader from Virginia. One day while George was hunting, he had an accident and was forced into a period of inactivity. During this time, he became fascinated with the marks white people made on paper. He called the papers "talking leaves" because he saw how people could communicate using their written language. George then decided he would create a written language for his people. After twelve years of work, in 1821 he had devised an eighty-five-character syllabary, which was adopted by the Cherokee nation. It was used to publish newspapers and books, and thousands learned to read and write the language, preserving an entire culture. Sequoyah, as he is known

George Gist, better known as Sequoyah, invented the Cherokee syllabary.
(COURTESY TENNESSEE TOURIST DEVELOPMENT)

to history, was part of the forced removal of the Cherokee to Indian Territory. However, his statue today represents Oklahoma in Statuary Hall in the U.S. Capitol.

FAMOUS TENNESSEANS TRIVIA

Q. What Jackson-born actor appeared in such movies such as *The Steel Helmet* and *Walking Tall* and the popular TV series *My Friend Flicka?*

A. Gene Evans.

Q. The character of Sergeant Carter in the TV show *Gomer Pyle* was played by what Clarksville native?

A. Frank Spencer Sutton.

Q. Andrew Jackson's wife, Rachel, had what "bad" habit?

A. Smoking cigars.

Q. Besides being Tennesseans, what do singer Dinah Shore, Olympic track gold medalist Wilma Rudolph, and Grand Ole Opry harmonica virtuoso Deford Bailey have in common?

A. Being stricken with polio at a young age.

Q. In 1937 what Nashvillian sculptor was the first African American to have a one-man exhibit at the Museum of Modern Art in New York?

A. William Edmondson.

Q. What Columbia native developed a serum to prevent cholera in hogs and also implemented the meat inspection program for the U.S. Department of Agriculture?

A. Marion Dorset (1872–1935).

Q. For what reason did the Memphis draft board grant Elvis Presley an extension before he had to report for army service?

A. To complete filming the movie *King Creole*.

Q. Tom Schulman, a former teacher at a private school in Nashville, won an Oscar for what screenplay starring Robin Williams as a teacher in a private school?

A. *Dead Poets Society*.

Q. What Roane County man was the first white man to cross the Sierra Nevada from the east and discover Yosemite Valley?

A. Joseph Rutherford Walker (1798–1876).

Q. For what oceanographic achievement was Matthew F. Maury, who was born in Virginia but raised in Williamson County, called "the Pathfinder of the Seas"?

A. Scientifically charting the oceans. (His book *Wind and Current Charts* formed the basis for all pilot charts issued by the U.S. government.)

Q. What Jellico-born singer and actress was in Irving Berlin's *Music Box Review* in 1923, performed on Broadway and on the stage in France, sang with the Metropolitan Opera Company in 1928, and starred in such motion pictures as *New Moon* and *Jenny Lind*?

A. Grace Moore (1901–1947).

5

From the Hills of East Tennessee

The Scopes Trial: A Publicity Stunt That Backfired

One of the most famous legal proceedings in American history had its beginning in the 1925 signing of the so-called "Anti-Evolution Bill." The trial, often referred to as "the Scopes Monkey Trial," was really a public relations stunt that backfired.

In Dayton, Tennessee, soon after the signing of the bill, some of the locals were sitting in Robinson's Drug Store discussing the new law and their town's ailing economy. Two of the men were Earle Robinson, known as the "Hustlin' Druggist," and George Rappleyea, the superintendent of Dayton Coal and Iron Company.

Rappleyea convinced Robinson and others to test the anti-evolution statute right in their own town, and they sent for the public-school teacher John Thomas Scopes. He'd taught many things, biology among them, but he wasn't sure if he had ever taught evolution. Nevertheless, he agreed to be a part of a test case that would put their town in the media limelight. Scopes was arrested and his trial, which lasted eight days, drew more than ten thousand to the Rhea County Courthouse during one of the hottest and driest summers in Tennessee history.

Adding to national and international interest were the leaders of the opposing legal teams. Clarence S. Darrow, the nation's most famous criminal lawyer, led the defense; William Jennings Bryan, a well-known orator and former presidential candidate, headed the prosecution. The presiding judge was Grafton Greene, a native of Lebanon.

Even though some of the legal team members on both sides tried to retain a sense of dignity and keep people mindful of the serious nature of the case, the trial was punctuated by comic interludes and showmanship. For example, outside the courthouse there were monkey souvenirs for sale, and one trainer brought his chimpanzee named Joe Mendi. The carnival atmosphere drew a record number of reporters, including the famous H. L. Mencken. The event was also the first American trial to be broadcast live on radio, aired by Chicago's station WGN.

Ultimately, Scopes was convicted, but the Tennessee Supreme Court overturned the conviction on the technicality that the judge and not the jury should have established the fine Scopes was to pay.

Joe Mendi, the chimpanzee who visited Dayton for the Scopes trial and contributed to the circus atmosphere, enjoys a cool drink at the table in Robinson's Drug Store where the publicity stunt was first planned. With him are his trainer, Gertrude Baumen; Earle Robinson, known as the "Hustlin' Druggist"; and Frances and Wallace Robinson. (COURTESY BRYAN COLLEGE)

According to historian Richard Cornelius, the publicity stunt backfired because "Dayton was made to look like a center for morons, anti-intellectuals, backwards thinkers, and bigots. The men who started the trial wanted publicity which would encourage investors in Dayton's potential, but this unfavorable publicity scared the fish away."

At any rate, their actions certainly put Dayton on the map. Even now, whenever the debate of evolution versus creationism comes up, Dayton, Tennessee, and the "Monkey Trial" are a part of the conversation.

"You Might Want to Do Something with This"

In the misty hollows outside Oak Ridge, this young boy loved to sit at his grandparents' feet and listen to their stories. They'd tell him tales of all kinds: pioneer stories, stories about their grandparents, and ancient folklore as they sat surrounded by the forests of the low lying mountains of East Tennessee. Sometimes they'd give him something old: a book, a farming

John Rice Irwin, founder of the Museum of Appalachia, gathered log cabins and buildings dating from the 1700s to early 1900s to form a village. Mark Twain was conceived in this cabin from Possum Trot, Tennessee (his family moved to Missouri before he was born). (COURTESY MUSEUM OF APPALACHIA)

implement, something that anyone else might have thrown away. "You might want to do something with this," they'd tell little John Rice.

From those beginnings, John Rice Irwin created the world-famous Museum of Appalachia in Norris. His collection of implements of pioneer life has grown to over a quarter of a million pieces, exhibited in a sixty-acre working farm and turn-of-the-century Appalachian village consisting of more than thirty log structures. The Museum of Appalachia has received accolades from such publications as *Reader's Digest, Southern Living,* and *Smithsonian.* According to the *Tennessee Blue Book,* the Museum of Appalachia is "the most authentic and complete replica of pioneer Appalachian life in the world."

Without realizing it, his grandparents gave John Rice Irwin a love of the past, which has served to preserve it.

The Incredible in East Tennessee

Gatlinburg has two interesting museums, both of which contain oddities, record-breaking items, and interesting facts. One is the Guinness World Records Museum and the other is the Ripley's Believe It or Not Museum. Here is a sampling from each museum:

Guinness

★ **Fastest rocket-powered street luge:** The current record holder, capable of reaching a speed of seventy miles per hour, was built by Billy Copeland of Ashland City.

★ **Most flying hours for a woman pilot:** Evelyn Bryan Johnson of Morristown achieved the record with 54,600 hours.

★ **Youngest to graduate college:** This record is claimed by Michael Kearney of Murfreesboro, who received his B.A. in anthropology from the University of South Alabama at the age of ten years, four months.

★ **World's shortest fire engine:** Owned by Fire Chief Henry Preston of Lebanon, "Little Squirt," as the engine is called, measures 118 inches long but is built to scale, and everything on it from sirens to lights and hoses works.

Ripley's

★ **Two-headed cow:** The stuffed cow is on display; when alive it was owned by Bobby and Gary Latham of Gatlinburg.

★ **Ham can violin:** This instrument was made by Fred Bowerman of Friendsville, who also makes violins from gourds and turtle shells.

★ **Holding a dozen eggs (unstacked!) in the palm of one hand:** The feat was achieved by Willie Camper of Memphis.

★ **Ordinance forbidding frogs from croaking:** This rule applies after 11:00 P.M. in Memphis, according to one of the cartoons in Ripley's collection.

The Tragedy at Mecklenburg

It's always a tragedy when books are destroyed. We usually think of this as happening in other cultures, but unfortunately, it's also happened in ours. Mecklenburg is one example.

Mecklenburg was the home of Dr. James Gettys McGready Ramsey and prior to the Civil War it was a place of peace, beauty, and stability. The antebellum mansion between the French Broad and Holston Rivers was not just Ramsey's home; it also served to store the archives of the East Tennessee Historical Society, of which Dr. Ramsey was perpetual recording secretary. Within its bookshelves lay precious one-of-a-kind documents from Tennessee founders such as William Blount, Samuel Wear, John Sevier, and Alexander Outlaw.

Dr. Ramsey had always been a states' rights advocate, and when the

Union Army occupied Knoxville, his stance led to tragedy. He lost a son in battle and spent the rest of the war in exile. When Union soldiers came to Mecklenburg and realized it was not only the home of the outspoken Confederate leader but also served as the library and museum for East Tennessee history, they burned Mecklenburg.

Dr. Ramsey witnessed firsthand how war destroys much more than lives and property. He watched, helpless and brokenhearted, as the torch was put to more than four thousand volumes of irreplaceable historical documents, books, and letters.

Itching for Justice

In Sevierville's early days, the town had no courthouse or other civic buildings. For lack of any other place in which to hold their judiciary proceedings, the people of Sevierville gathered in a stable. The stable had one big problem, however: it was heavily infested with fleas! Many trials were hastily performed as a result. One person wrote, "Perhaps nowhere else in Tennessee did the accused receive quicker versions of the speedy trials due them." The infestation got so bad that some of the attorneys finally burned it to the ground.

The Sevier County Courthouse, built during 1895–96, has not reported such infestations.

A Moonshine Story

East Tennessee has its own style of entrepreneurs—folks in the mountains who participate in the illicit production of whiskey, called moonshine. Cocke County was, at one time, the moonshine capital of the world, and in the Big South Fork National River and Recreation Area, the park service has estimated there was one still for every 116 acres of what is now park land.

The making of moonshine oftentimes has been a family tradition since the first settlers came to the mountains. After the Revolution veterans were given certificates allowing them to make and sell whiskey. Then their children took up the vocation, and so on. Some people believe that the exemp-

The first step in the making of moonshine is building a still. The illegal production of whiskey has often been a family tradition in the mountains of East Tennessee. (Courtesy East Tennessee State University Archives)

tions their forefathers enjoyed were passed down to them, along with their hair and eye color. Making moonshine, they think, doesn't clash with their being upstanding, God-fearing citizens; they consider the making of moonshine a right that is uniquely theirs.

Likker-Makin' Glossary

Carlock Stooksbury of the Museum of Appalachia in Norris defines the terms used by moonshiners:

Backins: when the proof drops below 70.

Bead: the bubbles that appear when you shake the "likker."

Beading oil: used by amateur makers of cheap likker, a high grade cooking oil used to put false beads on low-proof likker.

Beer: first stage of making likker, also called "mash" or "slop."

Branch: a source of water, a good place to set up a still so you will have plenty of cold water to cool the worm, or condenser.

Burner iron: iron pipe, one and one-half to two inches, with gashes sawed about one inch apart to let the flames come out and make a circle inside the core.

Cap: the part that catches the alcohol vapors that come out of the still.

Cap arm: the arm on the cap that connects to the horse's head, which goes from the cap to the thump post.

Cape: the part the cap fits in.

Case: six gallons of likker in one-gallon glass jugs, or twelve half-gallon jars. (Anyone who puts likker in plastic milk jugs shows their likker is not worth a damn.)

Condenser: same function as a worm, turns steam into liquid.

Core: goes through the lower two-thirds of the pot to put the burner iron and generator through.

Feints: removing leftover liquid in the thump keg, washing it, then replacing with fresh backins before the next run.

Flake stand: also called a cooling tub; what the worm or condenser sits in, with cold water piped to the bottom to push the hot water off the top to keep it cool.

Generator: a curved pipe made out of one-quarter-inch black iron pipe, which must become hot before the fuel will start generating; works like a Coleman gas stove.

High shots: likker that first comes out of the worm, 180 proof.

Malt: may be made out of corn, barley, or rye that is sprouted, dried, and ground to break down the carbohydrates in the grain and turn them into sugar. (Modern-day moonshiners don't go to the extra work and expense. They throw yeast in.)

Pot: main part of a stilling outfit.

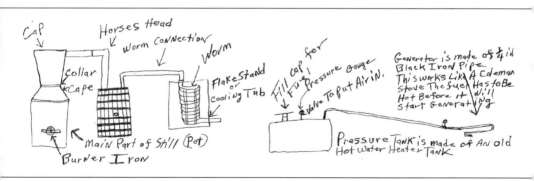

The person who rendered this diagram of a still claims to have no first-hand knowledge of liquor making, yet declines to be identified. (COURTESY MUSEUM OF APPALACHIA)

Pressure tank: fuel tank usually made out of an old hot water tank, into which is poured the fuel, half gas and half kerosene; contains a to gauge measure air pressure pushing fuel to the generator; also equipped with a tire valve to pump the tank with.

Proof: the amount of alcohol in your likker.

Tempering likker: occurs when the proof is cut down by adding water or backins.

Thump keg: gives likker a second distilling on one run, like a filter to catch any water or fusel oil (an oil present in the grain, mainly composed of amyl alcohols) to keep it from getting in the likker.

Thump post: a pipe that goes down in the thump keg with a notch cut out to let the steam through.

Worm: a copper coil, usually forty-eight feet long, that will hold anywhere from three hundred to six hundred gallons.

Worm connection: a pipe that goes from the thump keg to the worm or condenser.

Did You Know? Pigeon Forge is so named because of the huge flocks of passenger pigeons that would flock to the river, attracted to the many beech trees along the banks. Some said the flocks of birds flying overhead would darken the sky at times (years before Alfred Hitchcock's movie *The Birds*!).

Later, the river served to provide power for an ironworks built by Isaac Love, which operated until the 1930s. The river and town are named for both the birds and the forge.

The Melungeons

A mysterious group of people whose origin is unknown live in East Tennessee. They are called Melungeons, a term, some say, deriving from the Turkish *melun can,* which translates roughly as "cursed soul" or "one who has been abandoned by God." The Turkish term has its roots in the Arabic *melun jinn.* Others say the term can be traced to the French *melange,* or "mixture," referring to a mixed breed. Despite these linguistic suggestions, no one really knows from whom these people are descended.

The Melungeon people were first written about when explorers James Needham and Gabriel Arthur traveled to a region now a part of Hancock County, which was one of the earliest areas to be settled in Tennessee. In 1673 they reported seeing "white people which have long beards and whiskers." When exploring the same area in 1784, John Sevier and his party also came upon the strange group, described as having olive, or sometimes copper-colored, skin and wavy black hair.

The Melungeons lost their considerable land holdings to the incoming Scots-Irish settlers when in the early 1800s the government of Tennessee declared the Melungeons to be "free persons of color." As noncitizens with their lands gone and with no possibility of gaining them back by legal means, the Melungeons withdrew into some of the more isolated parts of the mountainous regions of Tennessee.

Although some experts say it's possible the group is a "lost Native American tribe" or people with a combination of African American and Native American blood, the Melungeons maintain they are descended from Mediterranean people. In January 1999 in Sneedville, the Tennessee Commission on Indian Affairs met to discuss loosening its requirements on who can claim Native American ancestry. Melungeon historian Scott Collins of Sneedville was there and declared, "We have worked for generations to discover who we are . . . we know Melungeons are not Native Americans."

Genetic research is ongoing to unearth more information on the origins of the Melungeons and how they came to be in Tennessee. With an international team conducting studies at Clinch Valley College in Virginia, perhaps more information on their mysterious beginnings will be discovered in the next millennium.

✪ Strange . . . but True

A World War II Tale

The U.S. Army colonel dressed in civilian clothes was on a top-secret mission when he walked into the office of Edgar Sengier in New York City. It was June 1942, a time of desperation for the Allied effort. The colonel was searching for uranium ore, the essential element in the making of atomic bombs. He knew it was a long shot that anyone there could give him a clue to help him obtain uranium, but he thought he'd ask this particular mining operator.

The colonel, whose identity is still unknown, was stunned to find the answer to his search right in Sengier's office. Within hours the military man had his uranium—one thousand tons of it!

This is the story of how the uranium vital to the success of Oak Ridge's atomic bomb project, called the Manhattan Project, was purchased from a Belgian mine operator, who had been hoarding it in New York City. A staunch anti-Nazi, Edgar Sengier was President of Union Minière in the Belgian Congo when he learned that scientists of the Third Reich were trying to develop an atomic bomb. If the Nazis got the technical know-how to make the bombs, he realized, they would soon be invading the Belgian Congo, where there was a wealth of uranium.

Unknown to anyone in Union Minière or in the Belgian government, from his mining operation Sengier began hoarding uranium, an ingredient found in the mineral pitchblende. He sent it in barrels to a warehouse in New York and notified some U.S. officials about his cache, but his message got lost in the mountains of government paperwork.

The colonel accidentally stumbled upon what he was looking for. The uranium became property of the U.S. government that very day, a coincidence that resulted in bringing an end to World War II.

The Weapon That's Been Used for a Musical Instrument

Long ago in East Tennessee there was a weapon that was also used to make music in times of lighthearted fun. It was the bow part of a bow and

Carlock Stooksbury has played his "mouth bow" for Tipper Gore and for audiences in Japan. He claims to be the only mouth bow player in the world. (COURTESY CARLOCK STOOKSBURY; PHOTO BY FRANK HOFFMAN)

arrow, and it was the only "stringed instrument" in America in pre-Columbian times.

Some enterprising Native American had found that by placing one end of the bow against his mouth and opening and closing his mouth while simultaneously plucking the string, he could get different tones. This music-making technique was passed on to the American settlers, but Carlock Stooksbury of the Museum of Appalachia claims to be the only musician who can play the mouth-bow with any skill today.

The Road to Nowhere

Near the quiet village of Townsend, Tennessee, just north of Bryson City, North Carolina, deep in the woods bordering Fontana Lake, is a road. You can travel this road until it ends abruptly at a long tunnel that goes underground for several hundred yards.

Its official name is Lakeview Drive, but the locals know it as the Road to Nowhere. Begun in the late 1950s as a combined project of the U.S. Department of the Interior, the Tennessee Valley Authority, and Swain

County (North Carolina), it would have brought more visitors to Fontana Lake and connected travelers with a more straightforward route from Bryson to Townsend. Because of a lack of foresight, however, a few problems got in the way of the road's completion.

Twenty-eight family cemeteries were in the path the road was to take, and people weren't willing to move their beloveds' remains to make way for a highway. Also, concerns about the environmental impact on the pristine wilderness around it stopped construction.

You can drive down the road and when it comes to an end, explore the tunnel on foot. Both the road and the tunnel remain as mute witness to our modern, ofttimes shortsighted, ambitions.

Jonesborough: Where Lyin' Is a Tradition

Remember how when you were growing up and told a story, your parents punished you and called you a liar? Well, if you come to Jonesborough you might be rewarded with applause and called a storyteller. For three days the first full weekend of every October, the town is filled with ghost stories,

Visitors listen to a storyteller at the National Storytelling Festival in Jonesborough, where lyin' is a tradition. (COURTESY STORYTELLING FOUNDATION INTERNATIONAL; PHOTO BY TOM RAYMOND)

outlandish tales, and unbelievable lore, in what has become the National Storytelling Festival.

It all started in 1973 when this, the oldest incorporated town in Tennessee, wanted to begin a celebration or festival that would not only help preserve oral histories and traditions but would also help bring in tourist dollars. A teacher by the name of Jimmy Neil Smith suggested a storytelling festival, and in an entrepreneurial stroke of genius, they named it the National Storytelling Festival, thereby assuring it media attention and future success.

The National Storytelling Festival is attended by all types of writers and tall-tale-tellers. The organization that produces the festival, Storytelling Foundation International, is located in the historic Chester Inn. There you will find a gift shop with various publications and tapes for sale.

It's the place to go to hear tales you might have told when *you* were a kid! No lie.

EAST TENNESSEE TRIVIA

Q. What type of architecture in farm buildings is seen almost exclusively in East Tennessee counties?

A. The cantilevered barn, with the second story larger than the first story, overhanging by about eight to ten feet.

Q. David Crockett was born in what town?

A. Limestone, west of Jonesborough. (Incidentally, there is no record of anyone calling him "Davy.")

Q. What county in the foothills of the Great Smoky Mountains received its name from the Cherokee word meaning "hazy" or "draped in fog"?

A. Unicoi.

Q. Since the 1990s what environmental role has Oak Ridge National Laboratory been playing?

A. Working with the Department of Energy to clean up and render harmless the toxic and radioactive wastes created in earlier years, not only in Oak Ridge, but in the United States and worldwide.

Q. Why was Tennessee chosen as the state in which to build components of the atomic bomb during World War II (in Oak Ridge) and later as the site for the Arnold Engineering Development Center (in Tullahoma)?

A. Relative security from German bombers and later from Cold War spies, in addition to adequate water and power supplies, access to rail lines and roads, and the availability of low-cost land.

Q. What designated National Wild and Scenic River that flows through the remote northern section of the Cumberland Plateau is one of the United States' last free-flowing (undammed), unspoiled river systems?

A. The Obed.

Q. In 1949 what museum in an East Tennessee city had its opening coincide with the removal of the city's security gates?

A. American Museum of Science and Energy, in Oak Ridge, where top-secret work had been done to develop the atom bomb. (The museum was originally called the American Museum of Atomic Energy.)

6

Religion and Utopian Communities

Stories of Snake Handlers

Differences in interpretation of the Holy Scriptures often lead to the origin of new religions and cults. One of these, requiring serpent handling, derived from the Gospel of Mark (16:18): "they will take up serpents." Mark also referred to believers having the ability to speak in tongues and drink "any deadly thing" without injury. Many adherents who participated in the speaking in tongues and drinking of deadly substances (including strychnine and lye) were members of the Church of God.

George Went Hensley is generally credited with introducing the handling of serpents in Ooltewah, at Rainbow Rock on White Oak Mountain around 1905. An illiterate, Hensley had led a tumultuous life as an on-again-off-again minister in East Tennessee who, in his backsliding days, had served time for selling moonshine. He was finally converted to the Church of God, which believed in the "following of signs," including handling serpents and drinking toxic substances, as part of its religious practices.

At Rainbow Rock Hensley prayed for a sign from God to tell him how to interpret Mark concerning snake handling. According to what he told his family, in midwinter, on snow-covered ground, a rattlesnake appeared and he picked it up without being bitten.

At a religious gathering in Owl Holler, Hensley began to preach and gained followers almost immediately. Some of his outlaw-type friends brought in a box of snakes, thinking this would discredit him. Instead, Hensley gathered up the rattlesnakes, water moccasins, and copperheads "like a boy gathering stovewood." The faithful saw this as a sign of God's approval, and other churches such as the Carson Springs Holiness Church of God in Jesus' Name, near Newport, took up the practice. Churches in West Virginia, North Carolina, and Kentucky followed suit, and Hensley became a kind of modern-day prophet.

A participant at a church service in Carson Springs handles a pair of diamondback rattlesnakes. (PHOTO © MIKE DUBOSE)

The practice of snake handling was considered bizarre by the rest of society. In 1923 the Church of God split into two groups, forming the Church of God, which disassociated itself from the practice, and the Church of God of Prophecy, which continued it. In 1947 the first bill making snake handling illegal passed the Tennessee legislature.

In his years of snake handling, George Hensley was bitten at least four hundred times, but in 1955 at a religious meeting at an abandoned blacksmith shop in Calhoun County, Florida, he refused medical treatment for a bite and died. The practice persisted and in 1973 the Cocke County judge George Shepherd tried and convicted two deacons for snake handling.

Believers continue the religious practice to this day.

The Amish: Living Apart from the Modern World

The largest Tennessee community of the Amish is in Ethridge, in Lawrence County. The two-thousand-member group can be identified by their clothing. Boys and men wear brimmed hats and pants with suspenders; girls and women wear plain long dresses, aprons, and bonnets.

Mostly they are recognized by the way they live. These simple folk regard modern conveniences such as televisions, telephones, motor vehicles, electricity and running water as unnecessary and even burdensome. Their main focus is the home and leading the simple life. An agricultural community, they are almost entirely self-sufficient. On the highways, their horse-drawn buggies serenely clop-clop along, as cars speed past them with their drivers intent on getting nowhere fast while fretting that their cellular phone batteries are running low.

This Protestant group broke away from the Mennonites in the 1690s and first came to America in 1728. The Lawrence County group came to Tennessee in the 1940s. Today the Amish live in twenty-three states and maintain their separation from the world. They do not go to war, swear oaths, or hold public office.

These simple, peace-loving people keep to themselves. Although their work on their farms is hard, by taking life more slowly, they seem immune to many of the ills of modern society.

Strange . . . but True

Gideon's Bible . . . and Distillery

Gideon Blackburn was a Presbyterian minister who had more than one talent. Born in 1772, he settled on a farm in Fort Craig in East Tennessee, opened the New Providence Church, and later started two schools for the Cherokee people living nearby.

His industrious nature didn't stop there. He also owned a distillery, and in 1809 the Creek Indians accused him of using their land to illegally transport his whiskey to Mobile, Alabama. This caused nearly irreparable damage to the minister's reputation.

He did recover from the scandal, however, founded other churches, and even became the president of Centre College in Kentucky. History doesn't say if he ever built another still.

> *Did You Know?* The largest religious publishing house in the United States operated by African Americans is the National Baptist Publishing Board in Nashville.

Hey, Man, Look! It's the Farm!

In the 1960s and 1970s, young people and visionaries from all over the United States took off in search of America and themselves. Some of them formed a community that became world famous: the Farm in Summertown, Tennessee.

The Farm is called an "intentional community" because it was settled with a definite purpose in mind. In May 1971 Professor Stephen Gaskin left San Francisco with 350 students and friends. After a seven-month tour of the United States in brightly colored buses and vans, looking for a place to establish themselves, they decided to settle in Tennessee. By the end of 1980 the Farm had become, in its own terminology, "the largest hippie commune in North America," cresting at around 1,500 people.

The philosophy of the Farm community is based on nonviolence and the belief that changing the world begins with the individual. In their tenuous first days, the newcomers were befriended by neighbors, who taught the "city folk" how to grow crops, use agricultural implements, and generally become self-sufficient. Since that time, the Farm's culture has contributed to the acceptance of a variety of lifestyles in mainstream American culture, including vegetarian diets, environmental sensitivity, global responsibility, and the resurgence of midwifery. Although its current population is only about 200 members, the Farm is still a thriving community.

The people of the Farm have also reached out globally, trying to help others who are less fortunate. They now manufacture books, videos, electronics, and organic foods. It is headquarters for Plenty, International, a global outreach relief and development organization founded by the community in the mid-1970s. Their projects include soy nutrition in Central America, support for native peoples through fair trade, and a summer camp for children from homeless shelters.

The impact of the Farm has been felt worldwide. Its members have improved the lives of impoverished peoples to such an extent, Mother Teresa was once asked to meet with members of the Farm when they were working at a relief center in the Bronx. Speaking to Nancy Housel, one of the original members of the Farm, Mother Teresa reportedly had tears in her eyes when she said, "Oh, the Farm and Plenty! You are the heroes of the world!"

Reverend Sam Jones and the Great Nashville Revival of 1885

In the spring and summer of 1885 Nashville was once again under siege, but this time it wasn't a Union army. It was in the form of a spiritual challenge by a nondescript, slightly built man who filled the largest churches and biggest tents with penitential sinners seeking a messianic conversion of themselves and their world. The collective soul of Nashville was turned upside down by the Reverend Sam Jones.

No soft-spoken, kind-hearted shepherd type, this Georgia native looked the ministers who heard his righteous tirades in the eye and challenged them as well. No wonder, he said, the churches were in such spiritual disarray, the people bewildered because they could not find their God. People were spending "all their time and all their money on the world," and "some people are actually ashamed to let the right hand know how stingy the left hand is."

He also turned his wrath on the church-goers in the crowds. There was no room for the unrepentant sinners at barroom tables or card games because self-proclaimed Christians had gotten there first, he told the galvanized gatherings, assuring the sinners not to worry, because "the company in the Church ain't good enough for them yet."

These insults served to create controversy around the evangelist, which was the best kind of publicity. The *Nashville Daily Union* printed an editorial saying that the citizens of the city known as the Athens of the South "are past the age of being ridiculed or abused into religion."

Rather than turning away from Jones and his abusive, coarse, insulting verbiage, the throngs embraced him. Alternating his sermons with exhortations, jokes, and shows of temper at "Christians who attended dances Saturday night and church Sunday morning," he kept his audiences never knowing what to expect next. When he compared his attempts to convert the city to the Confederates' brave struggle in the battle of Nashville, he won over hard-hearted men whose emotions were still in the 1860s. One night alone, five hundred stood up to dedicate their lives to the Lord.

One of these was "Steamboatin' Tom" Ryman. Ryman was a wealthy river man, with thirty-five steamboats plying the rivers. He was also said to be "a swinging soul who ran floating dens of iniquity." That ended when he heard Jones speak.

Ryman had come to protect his business interests, for Jones was speaking out against anyone who peddled or consumed the "devil's brew" and Ryman's boats often carried "old wine and young whiskey."

The crowds were astonished when Jones held out his hand, saying he knew Ryman and the others had come to protest his stance. He then asked them to take his hand. And Ryman, leaning on a cane, stumped up and did so, saying, "I came here for the purpose stated by Mr. Jones, and he has whipped me with the Gospel of Christ." Realizing that the new converts would need a more spacious place in which to worship, Ryman began building the Union Gospel Tabernacle in downtown Nashville, later known as the Ryman Auditorium and "the Mother Church of Country Music," one of the earlier homes of the Grand Ole Opry.

He Wore Out Some Horses!

Burton McMahan Martin, a McMinn County native, was a circuit-riding preacher with the Methodist Episcopal Church in 1898. He preached in churches located hundreds of miles from each other—Knoxville, Pikeville, Maryville, Athens, and Rockwood.

Did You Know? Compared to other states, Tennessee has one of the highest percentages of Protestants, including over one million Baptists associated with the Southern Baptist Convention. The state is also home to many other varieties of the Baptist faith, some of which are found only in particular areas. The pull of evangelism is strong in Tennessee, and if you cross just about any river on a Sunday afternoon, you'll find some church members there, baptizing their own for God.

Members of a church in Carter County performed this baptism in a local creek around fifty years ago. (COURTESY TENNESSEE STATE LIBRARY AND ARCHIVES)

The Story of Rugby

Thomas Hughes was an Englishman, former member of Parliament, social visionary, and author. His 1857 novel, *Tom Brown's School Days,* was popular both here and in England. It was based on Hughes's experiences while enrolled at Rugby, a prestigious British boys' boarding school.

In 1870 Hughes visited America and was enthralled with how relatively simple it was for a man of education to enter just about any field of endeavor he desired. He began to envision a place containing the best of both British and American worlds, one that offered the pleasant lifestyle he had always known, yet did away with the social and economic barriers imposed by British elitist society.

Hughes became part of a venture company composed of capitalists from England and New England, who bought land in East Tennessee and called themselves the Board of Aid to Land Ownership. In the post–Civil War period, the plan for a utopian society in which southerners (especially Tennesseans) and Englishmen would work side by side was an appealing one.

When Rugby was officially named on October 5, 1880, it already had around 100 residents from both sides of the Atlantic. By midsummer 1881, the population had grown to about 300. Buildings such as the Tabard Inn and Christ Episcopal Church had been built, along with lovely homes and a library containing first-edition Victorian texts. For a while, it seemed that Hughes's vision had become a reality.

Then in the late summer of 1881, typhoid fever struck. Although only a handful of people died, many others left in panic and the utopian colony dwindled to about 60 souls.

Rugby's numbers grew again, with the population rising to around 450, but Hughes's grand dream never fully materialized. In the new millennium, however, there is promise for Rugby. A Rugby Restoration Association has been formed, and Historic Rugby is becoming a popular tourist stop.

 RELIGION TRIVIA

Q. Established near Blountville in 1786, what was the first Methodist Church in Tennessee?

A. Acuff's Chapel.

Q. What was one of the main causes of death for the early circuit-riding preachers?

A. Consumption.

Q. What Rutherford County native was a Methodist circuit rider between 1825 and 1827, served as a missionary to the Cherokee Indians, and during the Civil War was in charge of Methodist missionary work with the Army of Tennessee from 1861 to 1865?

A. John B. McFerrin, who also wrote *History of Methodism in Tennessee.*

Q. Tennessee's oldest surviving African American church was built in what city?

A. Memphis (Beale Street Baptist Church, built in 1864).

Q. What place of worship in Nutbush is the oldest of its kind in continuous use in the state?

A. Temple Adas Israel, established in 1882.

Q. In 1796 Quakers from North Carolina established what town just west of Maryville?

A. Friendsville.

Q. What was the first African American church to be established in Tennessee?

A. First Baptist Church, Colored, of Nashville, in 1848.

Q. What Presbyterian preacher came to the vicinity of Jonesborough in 1780 and organized not only a congregation but a school which later became Washington College?

A. Reverend Samuel Doak. His church is now the First Presbyterian Church in Greeneville.

Q. What was the first journal in the country solely devoted to the anti-slavery movement?

A. *Manumission Intelligencer,* published at Jonesborough by Quaker Elihu Embree, who had freed his own slaves in 1815.

7

Sports

It's Football Time in Tennessee!

All kinds of signs indicate when fall has come to the Volunteer State. Leaves change, the air gets chilly and crisp, and skies clear. For sports fans, though, the one thing that meant fall was the voice of John Ward saying, "It's football time in Tennessee!"

For more than thirty years the man known as "the Voice of the Vols" gave the details of University of Tennessee football games and got hearts racing with "Touchdown, Big Orange!" and "Give him six!"

There are many stories about John Ward, but Nashville *Tennessean* sportswriter Larry Woody recalled one that revealed a little-known side of the Voice of the Vols.

Dennis Fitzgerald, who had been deaf since an early childhood accident, worked in the newspaper's composing room. His favorite sports figures were NASCAR star Richard Petty and UT announcer John Ward. Fitzgerald had known

John Ward, the "Voice of the Vols" for more than thirty years, set fans' hearts racing with his "Touchdown, Big Orange!" (COURTESY UNIVERSITY OF TENNESSEE SPORTS INFORMATION)

105

Ward's family for many years: Ward's father had been principal at Tennessee School for the Deaf, and Ward's mother had been Fitzgerald's first-grade teacher. As a grown man with a family of his own, Fitzgerald would attend UT football games with his son, who used sign language to interpret what Ward was saying over the mike.

When Woody wrote an article about Fitzgerald, the deaf man mentioned his sports heroes and spoke of Ward in the most glowing of terms. Ward read the piece a few days later in the *Tennessean*, and the deaf man's words inspired Ward to find his address and write him a personal letter thanking him. Fitzgerald carried that letter with him until his death some years later.

Recalling that one gesture on the eve of Ward's retirement, Woody wrote: "When I remember John Ward, I won't first think of football or basketball, of his descriptions of big games and thrilling victories. I'll think of a genuinely nice guy, a caring person. I'll think of class."

Did You Know? Tennessee State University's athletes have won twenty-nine medals in the Olympic Games. Some of those athletes are Ralph Boston, Wyomia Tyus, and Wilma Rudolph.

Peyton Manning: A Personal Glimpse

It was spring 1998, and the Vols were tired after practice. As Peyton Manning headed to the locker room, he heard a voice. "Mr. Manning, please sign my autograph book?" the youngster said as she held her father's hand. Manning smiled, put down his helmet, and answered, "Sure. What do you want me to write in your book?"

This is typical behavior of Peyton Manning. The former University of Tennessee star quarterback is probably the most popular athlete to come through Tennessee and is definitely the most decorated football athlete Tennessee has had. With the exception of the Heisman Trophy, Manning has been awarded every honor there is, including the Sullivan Award, which goes to the number-one amateur athlete in the United States in any sport.

Even his youngest fans get the same attention that the prestigious announcers and his adult fans enjoy. This responsive attitude toward his public has its roots in Peyton's early childhood. He is the son of Archie Manning, who was an All-American quarterback at the University of Mississippi and later played for the New Orleans Saints. Peyton recalled when he and his brother, Cooper, were growing up, after games they would go down to the locker room. "Come on, Dad," he and Cooper would say. "Let's go home and toss the ball around." As young kids tend to be, they were impatient to leave.

But Archie Manning showed his sons how to handle publicity. Postgame, Peyton would sometimes see his father tired or dejected in the locker room, but when he left to meet his fans and the media, he adopted the demeanor of the hero they were looking for, and he stayed until the last interview was done and the final autograph signed.

Whatever he had to do, Peyton Manning's father worked until the job was finished. This lesson by example has served Peyton well and is one of the main reasons he is so successful. "Once I became the starting quarterback at Tennessee," he has said, "and then when I came to the pros, I understood exactly what my dad was talking about—take responsibility for the position you have."

Peyton Manning learned from his dad's example how to handle the limelight. (COURTESY UNIVERSITY OF TENNESSEE SPORTS INFORMATION)

Smokey, the University of Tennessee mascot, pays close attention to the game. (COURTESY UNIVERSITY OF TENNESSEE SPORTS INFORMATION)

Now You Can Sing Along

Okay, admit it: you've always wanted to sing along at football games. Now, you can. After all, it's one of the official state songs.

Rocky Top

Wish that I was on ol' Rocky Top
Down in the Tennessee hills
Ain't no smoggy smoke on Rocky Top
Ain't no telephone bills
Once I had a girl on Rocky Top
Half bear, other half cat
Wild as a mink, but sweet as soda pop
I still dream about that.

(Chorus)

Rocky Top, you'll always be

Home sweet home to me

Good ol' Rocky Top

Rocky Top Tennessee, Rocky Top Tennessee

Once two strangers climbed ol' Rocky Top

Lookin' for a moonshine still

Strangers ain't come down from Rocky Top

Reckon they never will

Corn won't grow at all on Rocky Top

Dirt's too rocky by far

That's why all the folks on Rocky Top

Get their corn from a jar

(Repeat chorus)

I've had years of cramped-up city life

Trapped like a duck in a pen

All I know is it's a pity life

Can't be simple again.

(Repeat chorus)

(© 1967, renewed 1995, by House of Bryant
Publications; words and music by Boudleaux Bryant
and Felice Bryant)

Before Integration, an Almost–UT Basketball Star Is Born

Americans have come to recognize how discrimination does more harm than good. In the case of Oscar Robertson, if Tennessee had been able to keep him, he probably would have been a UT star instead of "Mr. Indiana Basketball."

Born November 24, 1938, just outside the city limits of Charlotte, Oscar fell in love with basketball at an early age. As a black, the only local high school he could attend in those days was Hampton Night School in Dickson, twenty-one miles away. Consequently, his parents took him with his two brothers to live in Indianapolis, Indiana.

Tennessee's loss was Indianapolis's gain: when he was in high school, Oscar led his teammates to forty-five consecutive victories and was named "Mr. Indiana Basketball." After high school, Robertson went on to the University of Cincinnati, where he made a name for himself as the "Big O" because he'd get so excited during a game he'd scream, "Oh! Oh!" Afterward, he played with the Cincinnati Royals from 1960 to 1970, then with the Milwaukee Bucks from 1970 to 1972, scoring a total of 26,710 points and making more than 9,000 assists during his career.

Although Robertson was short for an NBA player (only six feet, four inches), he was named College Player of the Year three times (1958, 1959, 1960) while at Cincinnati. In 1960 he led the U.S. Olympic basketball team to a gold medal. In 1961 he was NBA Rookie of the Year, in 1964 the Royals' Most Valuable Player, and in 1971 NBA Champion with the Bucks.

If racial discrimination hadn't caused Robertson to move away, would he have been a UT star instead of an Indianapolis one?

Did You Know? These coaches wore more than one hat! Robert Reese Neyland became a brigadier general in the U.S. Army in 1944, after serving as head coach at the University of Tennessee from 1926 to 1931. Jesse Neely coached football at Rhodes College (then Southwestern), Rice University, the University of Alabama, and Clemson University, after earning a law degree from Vanderbilt (he later became Vanderbilt's athletic director).

La Gazella Nera **from Tennessee**

Born in Clarksville in 1940, Wilma Rudolph was sickly and under-weight, the twentieth child out of twenty-two in her family. As a child she suffered from a variety of illnesses, including pneumonia and polio. As a result, she didn't walk until age eight, and then only with a leg brace.

Wilma Rudolph runs for the gold in the 1960 Olympics. (COURTESY THE *LEAF CHRONICLE*, CLARKESVILLE, TENN.)

Wilma began playing basketball with her older brothers and sisters when she was around eleven. She had been told to wear corrective shoes but preferred to play bare-foot. She ended up being a high school track and basketball star, qualified for the U.S. Olympic team in 1956, and won the bronze in the relay competition.

At Tennessee State College she played with the Tigerbelles, but various physical ail-ments sidelined her in 1958 and 1959. However, she once again excelled in the Olympics in 1960, setting new world records and winning the gold in both the 100-meter and 200-meter dashes. On a post-Olympic European tour, Rudolph was popular with the Italians, who called her *la Gazella Nera* ("the Black Gazelle"), and with the French, who affectionately dubbed her *la Perle Noir* ("the Black Pearl"). She was named the Associated Press Female Athlete of the Year in both 1960 and 1961 and was only the third woman to win the prestigious Sullivan Outstanding Athlete of the Year award, in 1961.

Rudolph retired from athletics in 1962 and turned her energies to help-ing underprivileged children through her Wilma Rudolph Foundation, which also sponsors youth athletic competitions. She died in 1994.

The girl who physicians said would never be able to walk, ran to beat her obstacles, and became not only the fastest woman runner in the world but was ranked the number forty-one athlete among the top fifty North American athletes of the twentieth century by an ESPN panel.

Best Streams in Tennessee

Here is a list, developed in consultation with the Tennessee Scenic River Association, of Tennessee's best recreational streams for paddling, canoeing, floating, and white-water rafting. The TSRA's website is www.paddletsra.org, for those who want to paddle online.

★ White Water Streams
   Nolichucky
   Ocoee
   Hiwassee
   Conasauga
   Tellico Big South Fork of the Cumberland

D. L. Hayes displays his record-breaking smallmouth bass, caught in Dale Hollow on July 9, 1955. (PHOTO © MIKE DuBOSE)

Obed-Emory System (National Wild & Scenic River System)

Piney River

Whites Creek in Rhea County Crab Orchard Creek

★ Pastoral Streams

Duck

Buffalo

Harpeth

Sequatchee

"Ghost River" section of Wolf River (a black water stream called "the
    Everglades of Tennessee")

Breaking the Color Barrier: Ted Rhodes

When Tiger Woods donned his Master's blazer in 1997, he thanked
someone very special to him. Woods had never known the man, but Ted
Rhodes had done a great service for him and other black golfers. He broke
down the color barrier to the "game of kings."

A premier African American golfer at a
time when such players were a rarity, Ted
Rhodes was posthumously inducted into the
Tennessee Golf Hall of Fame in Franklin in
1998 (he died in 1969). Rhodes won more
than one hundred tournaments in his career,
and CBS produced a documentary of his life.
Tiger Woods's commercials for Nike include
Ted Rhodes's image.

Ted grew up in Nashville, where in 1929,
at the age of sixteen, he was a caddie at the
Belle Meade Country Club, which banned
African Americans from membership. The
race issue in golf was first broached seriously
in 1948 when Rhodes and another African

*In 1948 Ted Rhodes (right) success-
fully challenged the PGA's
Caucasians-only rule.* (Courtesy Ted
Rhodes Foundation)

American golf whiz, Bill Spiller, were among the top winners in the Los Angeles Open and went on to play in the Oakland Open.

The rules were different in the Oakland Open, though. After a couple of practice rounds, they were taken aside and told by George Schneiter, the head of the Tournament Players Bureau, "This tournament is only open to regular members of the PGA of America." Rhodes and Spiller were, of course, not members because of the PGA's Caucasians-only rule. They were humiliated, but they weren't going to take their clubs and go home.

Rhodes, Spiller, and another African American player, Madison Gunter, joined forces. First they held a news conference in Oakland, then contacted a sports producer with ABC, who aired their story across the nation. Finally, they filed a $250,000 lawsuit against the Professional Golf Association of America. The PGA offered a deal: if the players dropped their suit, the PGA would stop discriminating against blacks. Rhodes and his two fellow golfers accepted, and in 1961 competition in PGA tournaments became open to all players, regardless of color.

NASCAR and Bristol: The World's Fastest Half Mile

In Bristol twice a year, the largest crowds of any sporting event in Tennessee gather to witness race cars going around the "World's Fastest Half Mile." What some of them might not know is that it's not really a half mile.

In 1961 Bristol businessman Larry Carrier constructed the track, an oval-shaped, perfect half-mile track. When it was first built, it could accommodate more than 20,000 fans, twice as many as most tracks.

It was originally banked at 22 degrees, but in 1969 the track was changed. Its new length measured .5333 miles, a little over a half mile, but it was now banked at 30 degrees. The track change was good for the fans because they could see all the competitors on the track all the time, and the increased banking, the steepest in Winston Cup racing, made the track faster.

Seating capacity now is even bigger since Bruton Smith's Speedway Motorsports, Inc., bought it from Carrier in 1996. You might not want to ask any of the 130,000 fans that can fit in the facility as they watch

Mark Martin, Darrell Waltrip, and others "swap paint" on the track if they realize it's not really the "World's Fastest *Half Mile*," because you might find yourself challenged to an old-fashioned settling of differences, Tennessee style.

Strange . . . but True

Taller than the cars whizzing past it, a bust of NASCAR-racer-turned-politician Richard Petty stands along Interstate I-40 outside Sevierville. It's a shock to come upon a larger-than-life bust, complete with cowboy hat, sunglasses, and STP racing shirt, as you drive along the interstate.

You Might Be a NASCAR Fan If . . .

The following items are all taken from real-life events.

★ You put off by-pass surgery because it's Race Day.

★ You help your mom get a job in a pawn shop so you can buy more NASCAR collectibles cheaply.

★ You have them bring a TV into the labor room so you and your newborn can watch the race as soon as he or she's born.

★ Your toddler knows all the cars and drivers, but can't yet spell his own name.

★ You name your dog Dale, your kid Kyle, and your boat Darrell.

★ Your room, office, or house looks like a NASCAR museum.

★ You started your own racing fans' website.

★ You go to early services at church so you can get to Bristol on time.

★ You plan your wedding service around Race Day so you can be track-side in time for the race.

Pat Head Summitt: Netting History

Pat Head Summitt was born in the Clarksville area in 1953 and spent her childhood helping her family on the farm, milking cows, cutting tobacco, and lending a hand in the family's grocery store. But her early life wasn't all work. She and her three brothers played basketball in the late afternoons after chores, in an old tobacco barn in which they'd built a basketball court.

The family moved from Clarksville to the tiny town of Henrietta when the budding basketball star was of high-school age. At Cheatham County High School Pat became a basketball all-star in 1966. While she was still in college at the University of Tennessee in Martin, she got a call from the University of Tennessee in Knoxville asking if she would take the job as head coach of the new women's basketball program.

During her first season the twenty-two-year-old novice worked on getting her master's degree while coaching her team to 18 wins. Twenty-four seasons later, her Lady Vols had won 664 games and lost a mere 143 and earned the title of National Champions in 1996, 1997, and 1998. In the 1997–98 season the Lady Vols went undefeated, something unheard of. Summitt herself has been driven to excel. She played in the 1973 World University Games, where her team won a silver medal, and in the 1975 Pan American Games, where her team took gold, and cocaptained the U.S. Olympic Team in 1976, where her team earned the silver.

Acclaimed as the greatest women's basketball coach in history, Pat Summitt was elected to the Basketball Hall of Fame in 2000. She commented that coaching is "about opportunities and taking advantage of [them] and not being afraid."

SPORTS TRIVIA

Q. What competition has its national tournament in Standing Stone every year?

A. National Rolley Hole Marbles Championship, where more than thirty teams compete.

Q. What model company town was established in 1900 for the production of cotton bagging and jute bags and even constructed a golf course and YMCA for its resident employees?

A. Bemis, which was annexed into Jackson in 1975.

Q. What Grand Ole Opry star once signed a contract with the St. Louis Cardinals baseball team and died in a plane crash in Davidson County on July 31, 1964?

A. James Travel "Jim" Reeves. (He was unable to play with the Cardinals due to a leg injury.)

Q. On November 8, 1958, when rioting took place for nearly two hours after the game, who had played the Tennessee Volunteers?

A. Chattanooga Moccasins, who won 14-6. (The *Knoxville News-Sentinel* reported that one thousand people rioted after Moccasins fans uprooted the goalpost at the north end of Shields-Watkins Field, resulting in police using water hoses and tear gas, with nine injuries and ten arrests.)

Q. Who was known as "the Mother of the Tigerbelles"?

A. Mae Faggs; she and Barbara Jones were the first Olympic gold medalists on the Tennessee State University track team in 1952, paving the way for Wilma Rudolph.

Q. What Vols player from 1928 through 1931 was said to be the greatest player Coach Bob Neyland had ever coached?

A. Gene McEver.

Q. What was the real name of the Chattanooga native who earned the nickname of "the Mad Bomber " as an All-American basketball player?

A. Richard Fuqua.

Q. Who won the Winston Cup for 1981 and 1982?

A. Darrell Waltrip.

Q. In what year did the University of Tennessee Volunteers first wear their orange jerseys?

A. 1922.

Q. In 1931 what Tennessee professional ball player broke the major league record for the most doubles in one season?

A. Earl W. Webb, with sixty-seven doubles.

Q. Where is the Southeastern 500 race held?

A. Bristol.

Q. Born in 1880 in Murfreesboro, what writer was acknowledged to be the dean of American sportswriters?

A. Grantland Rice.

Q. What is Tennessee's most heavily fished trout stream?

A. South Holston.

Q. In 1877 what city was the first to have a professional baseball team?

A. Memphis, with the Red Stockings, who lasted only one season.

Q. The Memphis Red Sox player Ted Radcliffe was given the nickname "Double-Duty" because he held what two positions?

A. Catcher and team manager.

Q. With what league were the Memphis Red Sox and the Nashville Elite Giants affiliated?

A. Negro Southern League (NSL).

Q. During the 1926–27 season, Satchel Paige played with what Chattanooga team?

A. Black Lookouts (NSL).

Q. For the 1945–46 season, what sixteen-year-old Chattanooga Choo Choos outfielder played without a contract?

A. Willie Mays. (His mother wanted him to finish high school.)

Q. In 1881 what was the first American-bred horse to win the English Derby?

A. Iroquois, owned by William Hicks Jackson of Belle Meade Plantation, Nashville.

Q. On what river were kayaking and other white-water competitions of the 1996 Summer Olympics held?

A. Ocoee.

Q. The stickball game that was a favorite with the Choctaw people ultimately became what modern-day competition?

A. Lacrosse.

Q. What hall of fame, the first devoted entirely to women, opened in Knoxville in 1999?

A. Women's Basketball Hall of Fame.

8
The Civil War in Tennessee

Frankly, My Dear, Maybe This Is Why Tennesseans Still Give a Damn

The War between the States. The Battle over States' Rights. The War of Northern Aggression and Southern Rebellion. By whatever names you've heard it called, the Civil War remains a source of endless fascination, even for people who are not history buffs. For Tennesseans especially, the Civil War is often still discussed as if it happened yesterday and not more than a hundred years ago. Perhaps one reason is that, with the exception of the state of Virginia, Tennessee had more battles fought within its borders than any other state.

The Mystery of the Headless Corpse

Colonel William Mabry Shy of the Twentieth Confederate Infantry was fighting with his men under the command of General Thomas B. Smith. It was December 16, 1864, during the battle of Nashville, and Shy and his infantry were defending the area outside Nashville then known as Compton's Hill. They were part of a Confederate line of defense that stretched for five miles.

The battle went awry for Shy and his men, and the Union soldiers succeeded in breaking the Confederate lines. The Southerners retreated to the Overton Hills with General Nathan Bedford Forrest's cavalry giving them cover.

General Smith was captured by the Union army, but Colonel Shy was killed in the battle. A friend of the family found him bayoneted to a tree, shot through the head, and completely naked. His body was taken to his home in Franklin, where he was buried. But that's not the end of the story.

In December 1977 some grave robbers opened Shy's grave. His casket was made of cast iron, but that didn't stop them. The robbers broke the front of the casket open using a heavy metal object, probably a post-hole digger.

In 1977 the headless corpse of Colonel William Mabry Shy, who died defending Nashville in 1864, was found sticking out of his casket at his Franklin grave site. This recently discovered melaineotype, a type of rare glass photograph, was probably taken between 1854 and 1856. (COURTESY LONNY MANGRUM, LOTZ HOUSE, FRANKLIN, TENN.)

Accounts don't say what (if anything) was taken from Shy's body or casket, but in the morning, police found a headless corpse with the torso sticking out of the coffin. They saw that the body was extremely well preserved, and they thought it might be the victim of some recent murder.

The body was given a cursory examination by Dr. William Bass, forensic anthropologist and head of the department of anthropology at the University of Tennessee, Knoxville, who searched for and found the missing head. For a short time he thought that they were conducting a homicide investigation because of the well-preserved state of the body. Finally, he determined for certain that the body was that of the long-deceased Colonel William Shy. "I was right about the age of the victim and the cause of death," he said. "I was only off on the time of death—off by about 113 years."

In January 1978 Shy was reburied with full military honors. His old casket is now on view at the Carter House Museum in Franklin. Incidentally, the hill he defended, Compton's Hill, has been renamed Shy's Hill in his honor.

Did You Know? In 1824 William Driver, a New England sea captain, named his U.S. flag "Old Glory." He later moved to Nashville, where, during the war, he kept the original Old Glory hidden in a quilt at his home. After the war, when Driver died in Nashville, the U.S. Congress made his grave in the City Cemetery one of the few places where a flag may be flown twenty-four hours a day. His family gave Old Glory to the Smithsonian Institution in 1922.

"Waterloo Teeth" and Civil War Dentistry

Before the advent of modern dentistry, teeth were more often pulled than saved, and many different types of materials were used in the making of dentures. Bone, ivory, and wood were some of the most common materials carved to make replacements.

Sometimes, too, human teeth were used, called "Waterloo Teeth" because they were often gathered from dead soldiers as they lay on the battlefield. During the Civil War, barrelsful of teeth were taken from dead soldiers, and shipped to England for use in dentures.

Still a Mystery: The Battle of Spring Hill

In 1864 the Confederate army under General John Bell Hood returned to Middle Tennessee, hoping to rekindle the South's dying flame and recapture Nashville. Fighting began at Spring Hill on November 29, and as darkness fell, both sides stopped for the night. The Confederates thought they had the seventeen thousand Union troops trapped, but inexplicably left the road from Columbia to Franklin open. Under cover of darkness Union troops marched past Confederate campfires 150 yards from the road and by morning were safely ensconced behind earthworks in Franklin.

General Hood, whose left arm had been shattered at Gettysburg and whose right leg was lost at Chickamauga, ordered his senior officers to meet him at Rippavilla Plantation in Spring Hill, where he gave them a verbal thrashing for allowing the Union troops to escape. Among them

was General Nathan Bedford Forrest, who blamed Hood, saying, "If you were a whole man, I'd whip you within an inch of your life."

Hood, who took large doses of laudanum to ease his constant pain, was so disabled some of his soldiers had to tie him to his horse. Nevertheless, the Confederates followed the Federal troops and the disastrous battle of Franklin ensued.

General John B. Hood couldn't understand how his men allowed seventeen thousand Union troops to slip through their fingers at Spring Hill.

To this day, it's still a mystery as to how seventeen thousand soldiers slipped out of the grasp of what should have been a tremendous Confederate victory. There are still heated debates about who allowed it to happen.

✦✦ Strange . . . but True

The young man was struggling with math. He already had a problem with too many demerits, and if he didn't pass math, he couldn't graduate. This filled him with despair.

Another student, seeing him struggle, offered to help him. The offer was gratefully accepted, and that was how the future General Schofield tutored the future General Hood so he could graduate from West Point in 1853.

Nine years later teacher and student fought each other, Schofield leading his Union army and Hood his Confederates at the battle of Spring Hill.

The Headquarters for Both Armies in the Same Day

The first person to build a permanent home on Lookout Mountain was Robert Cravens in 1856. It was a simple L-shaped single-storied home with six rooms. For some years, peace reigned at Cravens House. Then the Civil War came to Lookout Mountain.

In September 1863 Confederate troops occupied the mountain and for a time held the Union army in Chattanooga. Then on November 24, General Joseph Hooker's Union troops attacked Lookout Mountain. That same day the Confederate army made the Cravens House headquarters as they tried to fend off the Union soldiers. When the Confederates retreated in mid-afternoon, Cravens House became Union army headquarters under command of General W. C. Whitaker.

Cravens House is now maintained by the National Park Service as a part of the Lookout Mountain Battlefield.

Did You Know? The Chickamauga and Chattanooga Military Park was the first national military park in the United States. Established in 1890 and containing 8,200 acres, it is the nation's oldest and largest military park.

Button, Button, Who's Got the Button?

After Abraham Lincoln was assassinated by John Wilkes Booth, Lincoln's vice president took over to face the task of reuniting the country in the aftermath of the war. Himself a Tennessean, President Andrew Johnson did everything in his power to protect his beloved state and the rest of the South from the full vengeance of the victorious North. Everything he did, however, was suspect since he was a southerner—Johnson later missed being removed from office by only one vote.

Tennessee was under the strict governance of William Gannaway Brownlow, a Virginia-born Methodist minister and journalist. At one time, he and Johnson had taken the same side in the fight against secession. On every other issue, however, they were at opposite ends of the political spectrum. Brownlow succeeded Johnson as governor of Tennessee when Johnson ran on the ballot with Lincoln.

As much as Johnson was compassionate toward the Southern states, Brownlow was vengeful against those who had voted to secede from the Union. Although he backed government bonds to rebuild railroads and other infrastructure in Tennessee, his vengeance against Tennesseans who had remained true to the Confederacy was unflagging. For example, after Lee surrendered at Appomattox, in many states there was a military prohibition against, of all things, Confederate soldiers' buttons.

No Confederate soldier—whether he was just straggling home from the battlefield, the hospital, or a POW camp—was to wear his uniform's buttons. The buttons must be covered or replaced (and the rule did not consider that these men were destitute and without "button resources"). What a final humiliation it was for one returning, beaten and dispirited, to come upon a Union soldier who would cut off the buttons with a saber, leaving the poor Confederate in a state of near-undress.

Brownlow and his Tennessee legislature tried to have a "Button Bill" passed as law, which would impose a fine of anywhere from five to fifty dollars on soldiers who wore their buttons on their tattered uniforms. Fortunately, it did not pass, but "the Button Trouble" was one more festering wound Tennessee endured after the Civil War.

CIVIL WAR TRIVIA I

Q. What profession were New Yorkers Albert Richardson and Junius Browne following when they were captured and subsequently put in a Confederate prison for almost two years, until some East Tennesseans helped them escape?

A. Journalism, working for the *New York Tribune*.

Q. When did the Tennessee legislature ratify the Thirteenth Amendment, abolishing slavery, which was introduced in the U.S. Congress in January 1865 and became the law of the land in December 1865 when two-thirds of the states had ratified it?

A. March 1865.

Q. What was the first Union vessel to succumb to the Confederate *Merrimack*'s attack?

A. The USS *Cumberland*, which was named after the river in Tennessee.

Q. When John P. Buchanan was the twenty-eighth governor (1891–93), what law was enacted to help Confederate veterans in the state?

A. Granting of pensions for war service.

Q. Known as the "Boy Hero of the Confederacy," what member of the Coleman Scouts, serving in the Army of Tennessee, was captured and executed as a spy in Pulaski in 1863?

A. Sam Davis.

Q. What Confederate general, the last one to surrender, later became president of the University of Nashville and then a math professor at the University of the South at Sewanee?

A. Edmund Kirby Smith.

Q. When Franklin County considered seceding from the state of Tennessee, what state did these "Franklinites" consider joining?

A. Alabama.

Q. Concerning leaving and rejoining the Union, how is Tennessee unique?

A. Last to secede and first to rejoin the Union.

Q. What was the difference in monthly pay between a Confederate brigadier general and a Union one?

A. $14 ($301 for the Confederate and $315 for the Yankee).

Q. For what is Virginia "Ginnie" Bethel Moon, who lived in Memphis in 1862, noted?

A. She was a Confederate spy.

Q. The fall of Forts Henry and Donelson on the Tennessee and Cumberland Rivers in 1862 brought nationwide fame and a nickname to what general?

A. General U. S. "Unconditional Surrender" Grant.

Q. What was the first Confederate state capital to fall?

A. Nashville, on February 23, 1862.

Q. What Confederate general was killed at Shiloh?

A. Albert Sidney Johnston.

Q. What was the first great bloody battle of the war?

A. Shiloh, with casualties totaling 23,500.

Q. What Irish-born Confederate general who died in the battle of Franklin was known as the "Stonewall Jackson of the West" because of his brave stance at Missionary Ridge?

A. Patrick Cleburne (1828–1864).

Strange . . . but True

Fighting in the Buff

On more than one occasion, soldiers on both sides were obliged to go *au naturel*, such as when fording a deep creek. They'd roll their clothing around their guns and carry them over their heads when crossing rivers. Other times they'd be in this vulnerable circumstance when bathing in the rivers, just trying to wash a few lice off their bodies. Sometimes they would use this tactic as an element in surprising the enemy.

U.S. Colonel James P. Brownlow of the First Tennessee Cavalry once led an "in the buff" attack. In July 1864 he had his men disrobe, cross a river, and sneak up on unsuspecting Confederate soldiers. Union General E. M. McCook wrote in his journal of that day: "They drove the enemy out of their rifle-pits, captured an . . . officer and 3 men. . . . They would have got more, but the rebels had the advantage in running through the bushes with clothes on. It was certainly one of the funniest sights of the war, and a very successful raid for naked men to make."

The County That Left Tennessee to Go with the North

Times were strange in East Tennessee on the eve of the Civil War. Everyone from politicians to yeoman farmers talked of secession. Some felt it was akin to treason for Tennessee to leave the Union; others answered they were following in the footsteps of their Revolutionary War ancestors who wouldn't abide tyranny. For many regions the issue was clear-cut—but not for East Tennessee. This was a geographically and strategically desirable region with natural deposits of saltpeter and niter. East Tennessee also had its railroad branching from Knoxville into Georgia, Kentucky, and Virginia. The Confederacy needed East Tennessee, and the Union wanted to set it free from the Confederate grip. One Richmond journalist called East Tennessee "the Keystone of the Southern arch."

There were many East Tennesseans whose sympathies were with the Union and this caused hard feelings among neighbors and kinsmen. The war became a very personal thing.

When Tennessee voted to secede from the Union, the members of the Scott County Court convened a special session. To a man, the members voted to secede from Tennessee and even renamed their county the "Free and Independent State of Scott." Ellis O. Butler wrote of the bizarre incident this way: "The brave squires dispatched a messenger to Nashville to inform the governor and the state legislature that the former Scott County was now independent and no longer a part of Tennessee but, unlike the rest of Tennessee, still a loyal part of the United States of America."

Confederate soldiers quickly took arms against the insurgents of Scott County, but the men responsible for the county's divorce from the state hid and evaded the attacks of their neighbors.

The matter was not solved with the end of the Civil War, either. In 1866, Tennessee rejoined the Union, but Scott County waited longer to adopt a resolution to dissolve the "Free and Independent State of Scott" and "petition the governor and legislature of Tennessee for readmission into the state of Tennessee as Scott County."

Maybe it procrastinated a little or maybe it wanted to prove a point, but

Scott County didn't make a move to formally rejoin the state of Tennessee until 1986, 125 years after it had seceded from the state.

When Tennesseans want to prove a point, they sometimes take their time doing it.

Whistle-stops along the Underground Railroad

Benjamin "Pap" Singleton, who called himself "the father of the Black Exodus," made his way to freedom along the Underground Railroad, from Nashville to Canada. A Memphis mansion now called the Slave-haven/Burkle Estate served as a stopping place for slaves trying to gain their freedom via the Underground Railroad. Because of its labyrinth of trap doors and tunnels, the Bell-Herrin House in Jonesborough is also thought to have been a haven for fleeing slaves.

The "Secret Soldiers"

During the Civil War, many civilians changed their identities so they could take part in defending their respective countries. One of these was a Pulaski native by the name of Sullivan.

In 1861 Sullivan joined up with a close relative in Company K of the First Tennessee Infantry Regiment. With the rest of the infantry, Sullivan marched long miles, carrying knapsack and weapons, set up camp, and endured sleepless nights on the cold, hard ground. Sullivan fought in West Virginia and then in northern Virginia, serving under Stonewall Jackson.

Sullivan's close relative was wounded on the battlefield in Perryville, Kentucky. When he was made a prisoner of war, Sullivan accompanied him to prison. From there this "secret soldier's" records are lost in the mists of time.

Sullivan was Betsy Sullivan. Her relative? Her husband, John. Like every other woman living in the South then, her life was affected by the Civil War. Some women responded by caring for the wounded after battles. Other women hid Confederate soldiers in their attics or spring houses, or defended their homes from marauding bands of Union soldiers in the aftermath of battles. Others packed their families and what belongings they had left and moved on.

But women like Sullivan, whether they wanted to join their husbands or sweethearts in battle, serve as spies, or seek adventures home and hearth didn't provide, responded to the war by cutting their hair, donning men's uniforms, and keeping their true gender a secret.

In *Patriots in Disguise: Women Warriors of the Civil War* (New York: Paragon House, 1993), Richard Hall wrote, "A surprising number of women served in combat on both sides during the American Civil War." The unfortunate thing is that, like Betsy Sullivan, these "secret soldiers" have been all but forgotten in the annals of mainstream American history.

Strange . . . but True

Outgoing President Andrew Johnson did not attend Ulysses S. Grant's inauguration. General Grant had let it be known that he would refuse to ride with Johnson to the ceremonies, and Johnson continued to work through his last official day, calling Grant a "faithless liar."

The Judge Who Straddled the Fence

Montgomery County native West Hughes Humphreys couldn't seem to decide which side he wanted to be on during the war. He accepted a Confederate judgeship while also serving as a U.S. federal judge for Tennessee. The U.S. Congress impeached him for this fence-straddling in 1862.

All's Fair in Love and War: An Unresolved Murder

In February 1863 Confederate General Earl Van Dorn received command over the Army of Tennessee's cavalry division, to assist General Braxton Bragg. His command didn't last long, though. Several weeks later, Van Dorn was dead, shot in the head by Dr. George B. Peters.

It happened May 7 at Van Dorn's headquarters in Spring Hill, just after the general had returned from Memphis. After the shooting Dr. Peters was a fugitive for a short time. Upon his return he gave his motive for the killing as defending his marriage. In other words, General Van Dorn had been "carrying on" with Dr. Peters's "incredibly beautiful" wife, Jessie.

Although Jessie left her husband the day he shot Van Dorn, they later reconciled. Dr. Peters was never brought to trial, so the true reason behind Van Dorn's murder has remained a mystery.

They say, "All's fair in love and war." Maybe, with Earl Van Dorn, it was a little of both.

The Soldier Who Fought for Love

Colonel Harry T. Buford of Memphis had several goals during the war, one being to become known for courage. Buford raised a cavalry troop and came to be known as a courageous fighter, especially in the battles of Bull Run and Shiloh. Colonel Buford also served as a spy and special agent for the Confederacy. It was after the war, when Buford wrote a book on these experiences, that the public came to know the soldier's true identity.

For Colonel Harry Buford was not Harry Buford, but Loreta Velazquez, who had disguised herself to be near her fiancé. In 1876 she published a memoir to support herself and her son.

Did You Know? In Tullahoma one of the largest U.S. Army training bases during World War II was named after Nathan Bedford Forrest. Camp Forrest also served to house eight hundred alien civilians in the early days of that war. Later, it was used as a prisoner of war camp, and at one time it was home to more than twenty-four thousand members of the German Wehrmacht. Camp Forrest no longer exists; the site today is occupied by Arnold Engineering Development Center (under the auspices of the U.S. Air Force).

General Nathan Bedford Forrest: From Private to General

Indisputably one of the greatest leaders and military tacticians of the Civil War, Nathan Bedford Forrest, who was born in Chapel Hill in 1821, never had formal military training or experience prior to the war. He was the only man on either side to enter the war as a private and leave a general.

Possessed of an incredible fearlessness and determination, Forrest joined the Southern army as a lowly private. His Civil War deeds are many: he killed more than thirty men in personal combat, had twenty-nine horses shot out from under him, and planned and led the first major raids, in several Kentucky towns, on November 14, 1861.

One of his greatest and most remarkable military achievements was on November 4, 1864. Forrest led his men to Johnsonville, Tennessee, where they attacked and destroyed the Federal supply and munitions depot located along the river known as Trace Creek. This resulted in the fall of the Union-controlled town, and was the first defeat in military history of a naval force by a cavalry force. Since then, the state has created in the vicinity of the raid a park named after this military genius.

Strange . . . but True

During the Confederate retreat, as the Army of Tennessee passed through Cowan, an old woman standing on her front porch watched the bedraggled procession. When she spied a particularly strong-looking soldier, she yelled at him, "A great big stout man like you! You ought to be ashamed of yourself. If old Forrest was here, he'd make you stand and fight!"

The old woman was addressing Nathan Bedford Forrest himself.

CIVIL WAR TRIVIA II

Q. What Knoxville-born admiral in the U.S. Navy uttered the words, "Damn the torpedoes; full speed ahead!" during the battle of Mobile Bay?

A. David Glasgow Farragut (1801–1870).

Q. The Confederacy's principal army on the western front had what official name?

A. The Army of Tennessee.

Q. What was Nathan Bedford Forrest's occupation prior to the war?

A. Slave trader.

Q. What Nashville woman served time in the Tennessee State Penitentiary for being a Confederate spy, and after the war established Nashville's first day-care center, which is still in existence?

A. Fannie Battle.

Q. What was the name of the temporary "housing" that General Ulysses S. Grant ordered Chaplain John Eaton to establish for the destitute and starving slaves fleeing their masters' homes in anticipation of the arrival of Union soldiers?

A. Contraband camps, nicknamed "New Africa." Eaton established the first such camp at Grand Junction.

Q. What Civil War dentist from Washington County is credited with inventing a splint for treating facial gunshot wounds and pioneered the use of aluminum for dental plates?

A. Dr. James Baxter Bean (Bean's Splint).

Q. Shelbyville was given what nickname because of its pro-Union stance?

A. "Little Boston."

Q. What county provided both sides of the war with nearly equal numbers of soldiers?

A. Bedford.

Q. Of what general was General William T. Sherman speaking when he said, "I think [he] was the most remarkable man our Civil War produced on either side"?

A. Nathan Bedford Forrest. (Sherman also once called him "that devil Forrest.")

Q. The battle of Lookout Mountain was given what descriptive name?

A. "Battle above the Clouds."

Q. What Union general was nicknamed the "Rock of Chickamauga"?

A. General George H. Thomas.

Q. During the war, Tennessee civilians made do with dried sassafras leaves and okra seeds as a substitute for what?

A. Coffee.

Q. Confederate soldiers ground corn with their rifle butts, mixed it with bacon drippings, molded it around their bayonets to bake in the campfire, and gave what name to this concoction?

A. Swoosh or sloosh.

Q. Of the approximately 180,000 African Americans who fought for the Union army during the Civil War, how many came from Tennessee?

A. Around 20,000.

9

Wheelers and Dealers

The Chattanooga Choo Choo:
An Old Train Station Saved from the Wrecking Ball

The first Chattanooga Choo Choo was a passenger train that began running to Cincinnati, Ohio, in 1880.

Chattanooga's present Terminal Station was completed in 1909, designed by an American artist in Paris's Beaux Arts Institute. Its entrance inspired awe, with the Grand Dome resting on four steel supports 75 feet apart. It was an architectural wonder, spanning the entire 68-by-82-foot waiting room.

The last train rolled into the station in 1970, and for a time it seemed the grand old place would be sacrificed to the wrecking ball. Some visionaries in Chattanooga, however, decided to renovate the station instead, and make it a landmark for the city.

In 1973 Terminal Station reopened its doors as a hotel—the Chattanooga Choo Choo. It has since become part of the Holiday Inn family, but don't think that it hasn't kept its originality. Just walking around the romantic gardens and fountains, peeking into the train cars that are now used as guest quarters, and strolling the lobby lets you step back into time. There's even an old trolley to take you around the grounds, and many of the old train cars in the yard have been refurbished and are now unique dining establishments.

The following recipe helped make the hotel restaurants famous. Did I hear someone say, "All Aboard"?

Chattanooga Choo Choo Peanut Butter Pie

1 9-inch graham cracker pie crust

½ cup peanut butter, heaping

1 (4-ounce) package cream cheese, softened

1 ¼ cups powdered sugar

2 ½ cups heavy cream

½ cup toasted almonds

Cream peanut butter with cream cheese until blended. Add powdered sugar and mix well. Whip cream until light and stiff, being careful not to whip into butter. Reserve some of the cream for garnish. Blend remaining cream into peanut butter mixture, with about two-thirds of the almonds. Spread filling in crust, pipe or spoon remaining cream on top, and sprinkle with remaining almonds.

Chill before serving. Serves 8.

The Song behind the Train

Americans older than baby boomers connect the Chattanooga Choo Choo with Glenn Miller's big band hit of the 1940s. Mack Gordon wrote the lyrics to "Chattanooga Choo Choo," and Harry Warren wrote the catchy music. The Glenn Miller Orchestra first performed the song in 1941, and it later appeared in the movie *Sunset Serenade* and was sung by Tex Beneke and the Modernaires. During World War II, the song was popular in Europe as well as the United States.

Chattanooga Choo Choo

Pardon me, boy, is that the Chattanooga Choo Choo?

Track twenty-nine . . .

Boy, you can give me a shine.

I can afford to board a Chattanooga Choo Choo;

I've got my fare and just a trifle to spare.

You leave the Pennsylvania Station 'bout a quarter to four,

Read a magazine and then you're in Baltimore.

Dinner in the Diner . . . Nothing could be finer

Than to have your ham 'n eggs in Carolina.

When you hear the whistle blowing eight to the bar,

Then you know that Tennessee is not very far.

Shovel all the coal in . . . gotta keep it rollin'.

Woo Woo, Chattanooga, there you are!

There's gonna be a certain party at the station,

Satin and lace . . . I used to call funny face.

She's gonna cry until I tell her that I'll never roam,

So, Chattanooga Choo Choo, won't you choo-choo me home?

Chattanooga Choo Choo, won't you choo-choo me home?

> [Words by Mack Gordon. Music by Harry Warren. © 1941 (renewed 1969) Twentieth Century Music Corporation. All rights controlled by Leo Feist, Inc. All rights of Leo Feist, Inc., assigned to EMI Catalogue Partnership. All rights administered by EMI Feist Catalog, Inc. All rights reserved. Used by Permission.]

Opryland Hotel: Tennessee's "City under Glass"

This is a true city under glass, with its own power and water supplies, fourteen food and beverage establishments, and thirty retail shops, with a staff of nearly forty-five hundred. The Opryland Hotel was built in 1977 with six hundred rooms, twelve miles from downtown Nashville. It's now grown to nearly three thousand rooms with 600,00 square feet of meeting and convention space. The exhibition hall, called the Ryman, has 288,000 square feet and is the largest single-level exhibition facility in a hotel in the United States. It contains five ballrooms, the largest being the Delta, which covers more than 55,000 square feet and can accommodate nearly 6,000 diners or up to 12,000 people for a concert. Its golf course, the Springhouse Golf Club, is home to the Bell South Classic, which is part of the PGA Senior Tour.

Visitors can ride a flatboat in the Delta at the Opryland Hotel. (Courtesy Opryland Hotel)

There are nine acres of gardens under glass. In 1983 the Conservatory opened with over ten thousand tropical plants. In 1988 the Cascades area was completed, with three waterfalls from 25 to 35 feet tall coming out of a 45-foot-tall mountain into a 12,500-square-foot lake.

The third "interior-scape," the Delta area, added one thousand rooms to the hotel. It contains four and one-half acres. A quarter-mile-long river runs through it, with flatboats available for rides. The Delta is also home to the largest restaurant in the state, Old Hickory Steakhouse; the first and only Coca-Cola General Store in the country; and the only Ben & Jerry's ice cream shop in the state.

With so much to offer, especially with its fabulous decorations and seasonal entertainment at Christmas, the Opryland Hotel attracts enough visitors to maintain an 80 percent occupancy rate year round, an unusually high figure for hotels. It's a premier meeting and entertainment destination—the world's largest under one roof.

Here is a favorite recipe from the Cascades Restaurant:

Grilled Asian Mahimahi with Thai Curry Sauce

<u>Marinated Fish</u>

5 garlic cloves, chopped

2 tablespoons fresh ginger, chopped

2 tablespoons cilantro, chopped

juice of 2 whole lemons

½ cup rice wine

½ cup olive oil

¼ cup sesame oil

5 6-ounce mahimahi fillets

Place all ingredients in a bowl and marinate the fish fillets for one hour.

<u>Sauce</u>

2 tablespoons curry paste

½ cup diced fresh pineapple

½ cup diced Granny Smith apples

2 tablespoons chopped fresh ginger

¼ cup chopped onions

½ teaspoon chopped garlic

½ cup rice wine

½ cup apple juice

½ cup pineapple juice

1 cup chicken broth

4 tablespoons sesame oil

Sauté the fish fillets in oil 3 minutes on each side until done. Set aside and keep warm. In the same pan that fish was sautéed in, sauté together the curry paste, pineapple, apples, ginger, onions, and garlic. Remove from pan. Deglaze the pan with rice wine, apple juice, pineapple juice, and chicken broth. Simmer for 20 minutes. Add sautéed ingredients. Strain and pour over the fish.

The Mecca for Shoppers: Opry Mills

When attendance at Nashville's Opryland USA theme park began to decline, the management razed it and built in its place an incredibly huge shopping-and-entertainment Mecca. Opry Mills opened in May 2000 and features an IMAX theater, interesting shops such as the Gibson Bluegrass Showcase (where visitors can see the company's musical instruments being created), and exotic restaurants such as the Rainforest Cafe.

When You Could See the World in Tennessee: The 1982 World's Fair

It was an incredible year, with twenty-two nations, seven states, and eighty-nine international corporations participating in the World's Fair held in Knoxville. Some of the events at the fair included its opening by President Ronald Reagan and an appearance by comedian Bob Hope, who celebrated his seventy-ninth birthday there. Over 85,000 visitors attended the first day, on May 1, and by May 16, the entry gates recorded the millionth visitor. By July 15, attendance had reached 5,249,131.

The European Community (EC) had its first pavilion at a world exposition at this fair, and the first touch-screen computers were there.

For a season Tennessee was host to the world; they built it, and the world came.

Food and Drink from Tennessee

Here are the stories behind some favorite foods and drinks that began in Tennessee.

★ **Christie Cookies:** In 1985 former Vanderbilt football player Christie Hauck decided to perfect a cookie he remembered a neighbor used to make when he was just a kid. It took Hauck two years, but he finally came up with the Christie Cookie. He opened his first retail store on Church Street in Nashville; now there are more than five retail stores and the cookies are distributed wholesale to universities and other institutions. Hauck also has a mail-order service, so almost anyone in the world can have a taste of the now-famous Christie Cookie.

★ **Moon Pie:** The Chattanooga Bakery, founded in 1902, was having trouble breaking into the Appalachian market. One frustrated salesman returned from the area and reported: "They don't want anything we make. They want something round, with marshmallow inside, and as big as the moon!"

From this, the now-famous Moon Pie was created. It became an everyday thing for the average working man to go into a grocery store, buy an RC Cola and a Moon Pie, and have lunch for less than fifteen cents.

★ **Goo-Goo Clusters:** The Goo-Goo Cluster, the first combination candy-bar ever created, is made primarily of peanuts, milk chocolate, caramel, and marshmallow. When Howell Campbell Sr. created it in 1912 at the Standard Candy Company in Nashville, no one knew what to call the round candy bars. Campbell rode the trolleys asking people to make suggestions. Finally a "lady school teacher" suggested Goo-Goo, the name you see today emblazoned on the silver foil wrappers in red letters.

★ **Coca-Cola in bottles:** As late as 1899, Atlanta-based Coca-Cola was still sold only as a fountain drink. Then Benjamin Thomas and Joseph Whitehead of Chattanooga got together with Coca-Cola's owner, Asa Candler, and asked him for the bottling rights to the beverage. As a formality, they agreed to pay him one dollar, which he never collected. With another Chattanoogan, John Lupton, they began bottling and distributing Coca-Cola, the container of which was made to resemble a dress shape popular in that time, the hobble skirt. Coca-Cola is still bottled in and distributed from Chattanooga, at the rate of more than 30,000 cases a day.

★ **Maxwell House Coffee:** In 1872 Kentucky-born Joel Owsley Cheek made his own green-bean coffee blend and began selling it to hotels and other establishments in Tennessee and Kentucky. Finally in 1892 the elegant Maxwell House hotel in Nashville agreed to serve his coffee in its restaurant.

Cheek must have known his success was assured when in 1907, President Theodore Roosevelt was a guest at the Maxwell House. Upon tasting the coffee, he remarked it was, "Good to the last drop." That slogan is still the Maxwell House Coffee slogan today.

Joel Cheek's coffee endeavor was eventually bought out by Postum Company (later renamed General Foods) and is now part of Kraft General Foods. This traveling coffee salesman became a millionaire from that 1928 buy out, to the tune of more than $4 million.

Other Tennessee Goodies

★ **Mrs. Grissom's Salads:** Grace Grissom's chicken salad, potato salad, and coleslaw are still packed and marketed out of Nashville.

★ **Double Cola:** Charles Little of Chattanooga invented it in 1933.

★ **Brock Candy:** Chattanoogan William E. Brock started the Brock Candy Company, which may be best known today for concocting the nation's first gelatin-based "gummy" candies.

★ **Little Debbie Snack Cakes:** Created in Chattanooga in 1933 by O. D. and Ruth King McKee, and named after their granddaughter, Little Debbie is now the nation's leading snack cake.

★ **Colt's Bolts:** Started by Mackenzie Colt of *Hee-Haw* fame, this candy is sold internationally.

And Just in Case You Like Something Brewed . . .

You'll visit the right place for prize-winning beer when you go to Big River Grille and Brewing Works in downtown Chattanooga. In 1998 its Iron Horse stout won the top medal in the World Beer Cup Competition in Rio de Janeiro, Brazil. Its Sweet Magnolia brown ale took the gold medal at the 1998 Great American Beer Festival.

They Got Their Start in Tennessee

★ **Piggly Wiggly:** This self-service grocery, the prototype of American supermarkets, was started in Memphis by Clarence Saunders in 1916. (Saunders's 36,500-square-foot home built of pink marble is now the Memphis Pink Palace Museum.)

★ **Shoney's:** Yeah, it was the Big Boy himself. Nashvillian Ray Danner bought franchise rights for Big Boy from West Virginia entrepreneur Alex Shoenbaum. Danner opened Shoney's Big Boy restaurant in Madison in 1959.

★ **Cracker Barrel:** Dan Evins opened the first restaurant in 1969 in Lebanon, Tennessee.

★ **Krystal:** Founded in 1932 by Chattanoogans J. Glenn Sherrill and Rudolph B. Davenport, the Krystal Company sold its square-shaped hamburgers for a nickel, along with "a good cup of coffee."

The Largest Collection of Aluminum Cans in the World

The name of the town Alcoa is an acronym for the Aluminum Corporation of America, which began buying property along the Little Tennessee River in 1910. The company built a series of dams to make its own inexpensive electricity, which is one of the biggest costs in making aluminum. The factory itself was built outside Maryville in 1913, after which the town of Alcoa was incorporated.

It must have been like something from a science fiction novel: everything was provided for the workers, from schools to housing to grocery stores to playgrounds and parks, and everyone who lived there worked for the company.

Although the Great Depression brought trouble, World War II brought an economic boom to Alcoa. By 1941 it had grown so much it was one of the largest plants in the world. In later years, TVA challenged the city's hydroelectric business, and Alcoa was no longer at the top of the heap in the aluminum market.

Now it's no longer a town with a Big Brother attitude. Alcoa has opened its doors to competition and regular folks who just want to live there, and the company no longer requires its workers to live in its housing. Alcoa has a working force of more than two thousand people, making aluminum for beverage cans.

Guess Who? Born in 1887, a Knoxville businessman and one-time mayor had helped construct the Panama Canal and had been a hobo before he founded a construction company that built infrastructures of all sorts—railroads, highways, and dams—throughout the southeastern United States. However, he's probably most well known for inventing the Dumpster.

His name? George Roby Dempster. In 1964 he was awarded the U.S. Navy Public Service Award for the merits of the Dumpster.

Adolph Ochs: One Stubborn Tennessean

There's a bit of a stubborn streak in just about any Tennessean worth his or her salt. Adolph Ochs had that, plus what Northerners call "chutzpa." Born in Cincinnati in 1858, little Adolph was raised in Knoxville, the son of German-Jewish immigrant parents, and fell in love with the newspaper business. Even as a young boy, he had a dream to one day own a big, successful newspaper.

At age eleven, he became a newsboy and then a floor sweeper at the *Knoxville Chronicle*, and five years later, "Ochsie" had become a full-fledged printer. For a short while he worked with the *Louisville Courier-Journal* as assistant foreman of the composing room; he then took a job with the *Knoxville Tribune* where Colonel John MacGowan, an editorial writer, took an interest in him. MacGowan and another party invested their funds so Ochs could buy Chattanooga's newspaper, the *Dispatch*. Tough post–Civil War economics, however, caused Ochs's fledgling journal to go bankrupt. Ochs was back to square one.

Borrowing printing presses and in need of cash, Ochs put together a Chattanooga city directory through which he came into contact with many influential people in the area. He discovered the *Chattanooga Times* was for sale and boldly approached a bank for a loan. His determined demeanor resulted in a loan of three hundred dollars, and once again he and MacGowan worked together. When times were tight, Ochs used a kind of "company store" tactic, getting credit slips in lieu of payment from his advertising clients, and giving the slips to his employees.

Adolph Ochs, publisher of the Chattanooga Times *and the* New York Times, *came up with the slogan, "All the News That's Fit to Print," which is still on the front page of the* New York Times *today.*
(COURTESY THE *CHATTANOOGA TIMES*)

The newspaper was doing well until a land deal in which Ochs had invested turned sour. Instead of declaring bankruptcy, he decided that if one newspaper could make a little money, two could make more. He checked around and discovered the *New York Times* was soon to be on the auction block.

Ochs was without resources but not without what Tennesseans call "grit." Riding in a parade in Chattanooga, he met President Grover Cleveland and used the opportunity to tell the president of his plan to buy the *Times*. Before the *Times* was sold at auction, Ochs had put together a financial plan to please his stockholders (which eventually gave him controlling interest). At auction time in 1896, Ochs was the sole bidder.

Ochs put all his energies into producing the best newspaper anyone had ever seen. He stayed away from the "yellow journalism" style popular at that time, and came up with the slogan, "All the News That's Fit to Print," which is still on the front page of the *New York Times* today.

Did You Know? Politically speaking, Adolph Ochs's parents came from vastly different sides of the street. While his father supported the Union in the Civil War, his mother was a Confederate sympathizer—and a spy!

The Slave Who Made His Own Fate

Born a slave, Shelbyville resident Wade Gosling vowed he would make something of himself. In 1878 he borrowed twenty-nine dollars from a man named Albert Frierson and opened his first business, called the Great Variety Store. Then Gosling, a voracious reader, began to teach himself law and finally, as he put it, "stood a verbal examination and was admitted to the Bar." He became the first black lawyer in the state and one of Shelbyville's most successful entrepreneurs, holding more land than most whites.

Les Paul and Gibson Guitar: Two American Icons

Already a popular guitar player, in the early 1950s Les Paul was also a leading innovator in electric guitar design. Thinking that a solid-bodied guitar should have a solid sound to match, he attached guitar strings to a miniature railroad tie (a four-inch-by-four-inch piece of pine) and made the first solid-body electric guitar. He named this first model "the Log" and Nashville-based Gibson Guitar produced it. Today Les Paul is an active spokesman for Gibson, and the Les Paul signature model guitar is one of the greatest musical instruments of the twentieth century.

A Lemons-into-Lemonade Story about Gibson

In the spring of 1998 tornadoes ripped through parts of Nashville, destroying churches, damaging historic buildings, and uprooting trees. Some of the trees were on the grounds of Andrew and Rachel Jackson's home, the Hermitage.

While some people bemoaned the loss of the great old trees, Gibson Guitar Company went into action. Henry Juszkiewicz, its CEO, took the usable parts of trees and created guitars, thus commemorating the Hermitage in a unique way and making music from disaster.

Vice President Al Gore, who attended the unveiling ceremonies of the Hermitage Guitars, commented, "I would like to thank Gibson Guitars for turning the debris of devastation into beautiful instruments."

The Wheeling and Dealing Belle of Belmont Mansion

Tennessee women have a way of retaining their femininity while getting exactly what they want. Adelicia Hayes Acklen was a perfect example of this Tennessee trait.

Born in 1817, Adelicia Hayes was the daughter of a prominent Nashville lawyer. At age twenty-two, she married Isaac Franklin, twenty-eight years her senior. They had four children but none survived childhood, and after seven years of marriage Franklin left Adelicia a very wealthy widow. Her estate included four cotton plantations in Louisiana, 750 slaves, and a large farm in Middle Tennessee.

When she was thirty-two Adelicia married an Alabama lawyer, Colonel Joseph Acklen, who agreed to sign a prenuptial agreement allowing Adelicia to keep all her properties and other assets. This was unusual in those days. Together, they built the twenty-thousand-square-foot Belmont Mansion in Nashville (now part of Belmont University) and had six children, four of whom lived past childhood. Joseph Acklen increased Adelicia's fortune three times over before his death during the Civil War.

Alone again, Adelicia Acklen found herself facing financial ruin; the Confederate army, fearing her 2,800 bales of market-ready cotton would fall

LEFT: Adelicia and Joseph Acklen built the twenty-thousand-square-foot Belmont Mansion in Nashville. RIGHT: During the Civil War, plantation-owner Adelicia Acklen avoided financial ruin by negotiating with both sides. (COURTESY BELMONT MANSION ASSOCIATION)

into Union hands, threatened to burn them. Adelicia secretly traveled to Louisiana, where she negotiated with each side, unbeknownst to the other. The Confederates promised not to burn her cotton; the Union, to help her move the cotton to New Orleans.

She then slipped her cotton through the Union blockade and sold it to the Rothschilds of London, who paid her in gold. She made $960,000 on the deal. Three weeks after Lee's surrender at Appomattox, Adelicia traveled to England to retrieve her fortune.

Although she lost more than $2 million when her slaves were freed and had to pay taxes and exorbitant fees to the blockade-runners, Adelicia was able to retain much of her wealth, while most of the other wealthy planters in the South lost everything.

Hollywood in Tennessee

Los Angeles and New York City have realized for some time that the Volunteer State, known as music's "Third Coast," is also a great place in which to make movies. In 1997 music, film, commercial, TV, and music video production resulted in more than $4 billion for the state's economy. David Glasgow of the Tennessee Film, Entertainment, and Music Commission says, "Memphis can look like one of a dozen big cities. It's very adaptable. A lot of places in Tennessee can look like a lot of other places in the world." Regal Cinema, the world's largest chain of movie theaters, is also based in Tennessee.

So, what's been filmed here? Here's a partial list:

Raintree County (1956): Starring Elizabeth Taylor and Montgomery Clift. This movie was filmed in Reelfoot Lake State Park.

The River (1984): Starring Sissy Spacek. TVA flooded part of Hawkins County to make this movie.

Starman (1984): Starring Jeff Bridges. Much of this movie had footage shot in Chattanooga and Nashville.

Mystery Train (1990): Starring Masatoshi Nagase and Elizabeth Bracco. This film, directed by Jim Jarmusch, takes a look at some of the more colorful characters of Memphis. It was one of the first widely distributed independent films shot there.

Days of Thunder (1991): Starring Tom Cruise. This movie was filmed at the Bristol Motor Speedway.

The Firm (1993): Starring Tom Cruise, Hal Holbrooke, Gene Hackman, and Holly Hunter. *The Client* (1994): Starring Susan Sarandon and Tommy Lee Jones. Both based on John Grisham novels, these films were shot in Memphis.

Love Potion No. Nine (1993): Starring Sandra Bullock. Chattanooga provided the set for this film.

Against the Wall (1994): Starring Kyle MacLachlan. Clarksville simulated the town of Attica, New York, in this made-for-HBO movie.

Rudyord Kipling's The Jungle Book (1994): Starring John Cleese. About 80 percent of the location shooting for this live-action Disney film, set in India, was done in Fall Creek Falls State Park in Middle Tennessee.

The Specialist (1995): Starring Sylvester Stallone and Sharon Stone. The first twenty minutes of the movie (when the dam is blown up) were shot at Fall Creek Falls State Park, simulating Colombia in South America.

The People vs. Larry Flynt (1997): Starring Woody Harrelson, Edward

Norton, and Courtney Love. This film was shot in the same lake and swamp area of Reelfoot Lake State Park as *Raintree Country*.

U.S. Marshalls (1998): Starring Tommy Lee Jones and Wesley Snipes. The chase scene through the swamp in this film was also shot in Reelfoot Lake State Park.

In Dreams (1999): Starring Annette Bening. The critical scene at the dam in this movie was filmed in Blount County.

The Green Mile (1999): Starring Tom Hanks. This movie was filmed at the old Tennessee State Penitentiary in Nashville.

October Sky (1999): Starring Laura Dern. This movie was shot in six counties around Knoxville.

Hatch Showprints

One of the oldest poster-making companies in the country still operates in Nashville at 316 Broadway. The company was founded by C. R. and H. H. Hatch in 1879. In the 1920s Will T. Hatch hand-carved the woodblocks used in the letterpress process. Many a country music fan and memorabilia collector has at least one Hatch Showprint, whose clients include the Grand Ole Opry and many of its artists. The Hatch brothers were fond of saying, "Advertising without posters is like fishing without worms."

McKissack and McKissack Architectural Firm: Story of Another Moses

In a story sounding like a page right out of Alex Haley's *Roots*, a young man of the West African Ashanti tribe was taken from his homeland and sold into slavery. "Moses," as he was called, was purchased by William McKissack of North Carolina.

As was the tradition then, the young slave took his master's last name. Moses McKissack was interested in building and became a master builder. After he married and had children, he taught his sons the building trade. His sons taught their own sons. Moses McKissack III took the skills he'd inherited from his grandfather a step further and in 1905 moved to Nashville, where he opened his own construction business. Word of his skill spread, as he constructed buildings for Vanderbilt University and the Carnegie Library at Fisk University. Through advertising and word-of-mouth, the grandson of a slave was designing buildings for clients throughout the state.

When his brother Calvin joined him, they formed McKissack & McKissack, Tennessee's first and the nation's oldest professional African American architectural firm.

After Moses III died, the reins were taken by his wife, Leatrice Buchanan McKissack, and daughters, who opened satellite offices in Memphis, Washington, D.C., and New York City.

Strange . . . but True

Tighten Your Corset!
Here's a Really Weird Story about TVA.

Little did President Franklin D. Roosevelt know when he presented his bold plan for the new economy in 1933 that some of his "dam plans" would go awry, but not for lack of a girdle.

As part of Roosevelt's First One Hundred Days of the New Deal, the Tennessee Valley Authority proposed to do away with flooding by building a series of dams. The dams would also help the economy of the poverty-ridden region by improving living conditions.

By the end of World War II, TVA had built sixteen dams along the Tennessee River and its tributaries and had purchased five others from the U.S. Corps of Engineers. From this, TVA had created fourteen million acres of flood storage and by 1946 was providing electricity to nearly 700,000 households, where previously there had been no power supply.

In preventing flooding in the Tennessee Basin, malaria and other diseases were brought to a halt. Economically, many of the people were better off, although there were some who spoke bitterly of losing their lands to the government agency.

Unfortunately, there was a problem with one of the older dams bought from a local power company. Hales Bar Dam leaked because of problems with the limestone foundation. There was so much flooding, some people said there was more water leaking out from under the dam than there was flowing over it. A construction firm was called in and decided to try something innovative to stop the leak. It dumped truckloads of women's corsets into the water above the dam, hoping the suction would pull the corsets against the face of the dam and stop the leaks.

It didn't work. Eventually, TVA dynamited the dam in 1968 and replaced it with Nickajack Dam, a few miles downstream.

The "Black Patch War"

In Middle Tennessee, tobacco has been a major source of income for farmers and those who deal in the buying and selling of the dark leaf. In the first decade of the 1900s, the tobacco industry was stained with acts of violence and oppression known as the "Black Patch War" (*black patch* refers to the region of the state that grows dark-fired tobacco).

Falling tobacco prices starting back in the 1890s caused some tobacco farmers to form an alliance to market tobacco more effectively, called the Dark Tobacco District Planters' Protective Association of Kentucky and Tennessee (PPA). Some growers refused to join the PPA; the PPA then gave them the derogatory name "hillbillies." The buyers' monopoly, headed by the American Tobacco Company, was termed "the Trust" by the PPA. The stage was set for violence, and some growers took to vigilante-type acts to attempt to coerce non-PPA growers to join the ranks.

In Robertson County, PPA members adopted the "Resolution of the committee of the Possum Hunters Organization," which aired their grievances against "the Trust" and "the hillbillies" and outlined their plan to "visit" both in the area. They planned on visiting in bands, to "convince" both groups to join them.

Their "convincing" methods became violent, and over the next several years, vigilantism by groups called "the Silent Brigade" and the "Inner Circle" included the use of dynamite, fire, and assault on people, their crops, and their farm animals. In Kentucky, several towns were taken over by these violent PPA members, and nonaffiliated tobacco growers in Montgomery and Robertson Counties, Tennessee, slept little at night.

The violence did result in the price of tobacco being raised, but much of the trouble was effectively ended by the presence of troops in trouble spots and by the lawsuits against the individuals involved. World War I, which caused the European tobacco markets for dark-fired tobacco to close, was the final blow to the PPA's existence.

WHEELERS AND DEALERS TRIVIA

Q. What popular home medical guide, first published in 1830 in Knoxville, became so popular with frontier and rural families that it remained in print until the 1920s and Mark Twain and John Steinbeck quoted from it in their novels (*Huckleberry Finn* and *East of Eden*)?

A. *Gunn's Domestic Medicine*, by Dr. John C. Gunn.

Q. Starting in 1884, why did the Tennessee Coal and Iron Company begin making annual lease payments of $101,000 to the state?

A. For the use of convicts as "free labor" instead of having to pay union miners. (The convict lease system as a government business subsidy was dropped after the union workers employed violence to halt it, in the insurrections of 1893–96.)

Q. What entertainer/philanthropist for years raised funds for St. Jude's Children's Research Hospital in Memphis?

A. Danny Thomas.

Q. From his Nashville-based studio, what celebrity regalia designer, who uses only one name, designed the Lone Ranger's outfit?

A. Manuel.

Q. What product did Samuel McSpadden, a manufacturer in Jefferson County, send to General Andrew Jackson to help him during the Battle of New Orleans in the War of 1812?

A. Gun powder from his mill.

Q. When the *Phoenix* was first published as a bilingual newspaper, in 1828 in Brainerd, Hamilton County, what two languages were represented on its pages?

A. Cherokee and English.

Q. What newspaperman and entrepreneur originated Chattanooga's Lookout Mountain Park?

A. Adolph Ochs.

Q. What is the nation's oldest, continuously operated African American bank?

A. Nashville's Citizens Bank, established in 1904 by members of the National Negro Business League.

Q. In 1953 what Madison company, a maker of pedal steel guitars,

Q. What thirty-two-story structure, used for sports, entertainment, and exhibitions, links a Tennessee city with the capital of ancient Egypt?

A. The Pyramid, in Memphis.

became part of the large instrument-manufacturing corporation Baldwin, Inc.?

A. Sho-Bud, founded by Harold B. "Shot" Jackson and Buddy Emmons.

Q. Nashville has been home to what well-known vacuum-bottle and lunch-box company since 1949?

A. Aladdin Industries.

Q. What is Tennessee's most valuable agricultural crop?

A. Soybeans, celebrated in Martin, Tennessee, at the annual Soybean Festival in September.

Q. What major international shipping company was established in Memphis in 1973?

A. Federal Express.

10
The Sound of Tennessee

The Birthplace of Rock 'n' Roll

Just thinking about the famous voices who have sung and recorded within the walls of Sun Studio in Memphis and the music that was played there is enough to give a visitor goose bumps. The walls are lined with memorabilia of artists who recorded there, including Elvis Presley, U2, Carl

Sun Studio in Memphis is said to be the birthplace of rock 'n' roll. Artists such as Elvis Presley, Jerry Lee Lewis, and Roy Orbison recorded here. (Courtesy Memphis Convention & Visitors Bureau)

Perkins, Johnny Cash, Def Leppard, Tom Petty, Jerry Lee Lewis, Roy Orbison, B. B. King, Howlin' Wolf, Ike Turner, and Paul Simon. "If it hadn't been for what happened at Sun Studio," Ringo Starr once said, "there wouldn't have been a Beatles."

Sun Studio gives tours seven days a week, all day long. Also, you can make your own recording, with the aid of computers and CD-music backup.

Barbara Mandrell Entertains the Boys

When Opry star Barbara Mandrell was a teenager, she and her family left their home in California to entertain the soldiers at military bases. When she and her mother, Mary, had to take makeshift baths in crude shelters outdoors, they took it in stride, until they realized they were being spied upon by soldiers! Undaunted, Barbara's mother said matter-of-factly, "Well, we came over here to entertain the boys, and I guess that's what we've done!"

Strange . . . but True

The Exchange

W. C. Handy's first musical instrument of choice was not the piano, the violin, or the horn, although he became proficient at all three. When he was eight years old, he bought his first musical instrument, a guitar. His father, a preacher who disapproved of musicians, made Handy take the guitar back to the store and exchange it for a dictionary.

W. C. Handy and Beale Street

A native of Florence, Alabama, William Christopher Handy was living in a small shotgun house at 325 Beale Street in Memphis and was working as a band leader and cornet player when in 1909 he wrote the campaign song for E. H. Crump, who was running for mayor of Memphis. It was later entitled "Memphis Blues" and in 1912 was the first blues composition ever published. Two years later he wrote "St. Louis Blues," possibly the most popular blues song of all time.

Derived from field hollers sung by slaves, blues became a popular musical form and aspiring musicians came in droves to Beale Street to learn to play the blues and perhaps make names for themselves. Then the depression brought hard times, nightspots closed, the musicians went north, and Beale Street sank into a seedy travesty of its former self.

In the 1970s some savvy Memphians recognized what a tourist draw Beale Street could be and launched a redevelopment campaign. Among the many attractions on Beale Street are the W. C. Handy Home; the Orpheum Theater for the performing arts; the New Daisy Theater, which hosts everything from musicians to boxing matches; and the famous dry-goods store A. Schwab. The old honky-tonk bars and pawnshops are being revitalized into new restaurants, shops, and nightspots.

Composer George Gershwin, who wrote *Rhapsody in Blue*, once told W. C. Handy, "Your work is the grandfather of mine." Now a statue of the "Father of the Blues" smiles over everyone in W. C. Handy Park, and a "whole lotta shaking" is still going on.

A local blues musician performs outside a Beale Street café. (Courtesy Memphis Convention & Visitors Bureau)

Did You Know? A music store owner tricked W. C. Handy out of the rights to his song "Memphis Blues." He told Handy the song wasn't selling well and bought it from the "Father of the Blues" for one hundred dollars. Handy got his rights back later when he discovered the ruse.

The Grand Ole Opry

It all began in 1925 as a local radio program called *Barn Dance,* and every Saturday night, more and more area listeners gathered around their crystal sets to hear country music played from the WSM studio in Nashville. To miss that show was like having fried eggs without grits for breakfast.

WSM attained network status in 1939, and the show, now known as the Grand Ole Opry, could be heard all over the U.S. As more people came to see the live performances, the Opry outgrew WSM studios. In 1941 it moved to the Ryman Auditorium. In 1943 the Acuff-Rose Publishing Company was founded by Roy Acuff and Fred Rose, and in 1945 Decca began recording country music at Studio B, WSM Radio. Country music had made its mark, so much so that on Okinawa it is said that one Japanese banzai battle cry was, "To hell with Roosevelt; to hell with Babe Ruth; to hell with Roy Acuff."

The Opry has been successful because of the music that comes from the heart and the musicians that have played from theirs. They've written and sung about love, lost and found; about dying parents, sweethearts, or children; about driving trucks or trains; about being lonesome, hungry, heartbroken, imprisoned, and otherwise wretched. Deep in "Bible Belt Country," they've also sung about their love of Jesus and waiting to see loved ones gone on to the Other Side. Songs going out into radio land (and later TV land) from the Grand Ole Opry touched hearts and brought tears to eyes because so many people could relate to the words being sung.

Lots of Opry fans came to be onstage themselves. Loretta Lynn, who first listened to the radio as a poor coal miner's daughter from Van Leer, is one. Dolly Parton, Floyd Tillman, Hank Snow, Tammy Wynette, Charlie Walker, Barbara Mandrell, Roy Acuff, Kitty Wells, Hank Williams, Patsy Cline, and more all made their mark on Opry history. Sara Ophelia Cannon—you know her as Minnie Pearl—was a regular comedienne at the Opry.

In 1974 the Opry moved to the auditorium built especially for it at Opryland USA. Since Decca began recording in Nashville, many other studios and related recording businesses have followed. What turned Nashville into Music City, USA, began with a small Saturday-night broadcast and celebrated its seventy-fifth birthday in 2000.

So You Want to Be in the Opry . . .

An official at the Grand Ole Opry had this to say regarding membership requirements: "A member of the Opry is inducted by showing interest that being a part of the Opry is important to him or her, both musically and to their career. They don't really have to audition because by the time they're inducted, they have already played the Opry several times. They must have a desire to be a member and a commitment to make appearances, but there is really no set number of performances required by the Opry." Hey, does that sound democratic or what?

Roll Call: Grand Ole Opry Members

Here's a current list of members of the Grand Ole Opry, with the years they were inducted.

1948	Little Jimmy Dickens	1956	Jimmy C. Newman
1953	Bill Carlisle	1957	Wilma Lee Cooper
1953	Teddy Wilburn	1957	Porter Wagoner
1955	Charlie Louvin	1958	Roy Drusky
1955	Jean Shepard	1958	Don Gibson

1959	Skeeter Davis	1982	Ricky Skaggs
1959	Billy Grammer	1984	Lorrie Morgan
1960	George Hamilton IV	1984	The Whites
1960	Hank Locklin	1985	Johnny Russell
1960	Billy Walker	1986	Mel McDaniel
1961	Bill Anderson	1986	Reba McEntire
1962	Loretta Lynn	1986	Randy Travis
1963	Jim Ed Brown	1987	Roy Clark
1964	Ernie Ashworth	1988	Patty Loveless
1964	Jim & Jesse	1988	Ricky Van Shelton
1964	The Osborne Brothers	1989	Holly Dunn
1966	Ray Pillow	1990	Garth Brooks
1966	Del Reeves	1990	Mike Snider
1967	Jack Greene	1991	Clint Black
1967	Stu Phillips	1991	Vince Gill
1967	Jeannie Seely	1991	Alan Jackson
1967	Charlie Walker	1992	Emmylou Harris
1969	Stonewall Jackson	1992	Marty Stuart
1969	George Jones	1992	Travis Tritt
1969	Dolly Parton	1993	Joe Diffie
1971	Jan Howard	1993	Alison Krauss
1971	Connie Smith	1993	Charley Pride
1972	Barbara Mandrell	1994	Hal Ketchum
1973	Jeanne Pruett	1995	Bashful Brother Oswald
1976	The Gatlins	1995	Martina McBride
1976	Ronnie Milsap	1996	Steve Wariner
1980	Tom T. Hall	1997	Johnny Paycheck
1980	The Melvin Sloan Dancers	1998	Diamond Rio
1981	John Conlee	1999	Trisha Yearwood
1982	Riders in the Sky	2000	Ralph Stanley

⬢ Stɾɑn©e . . . but True

The Boy Who Didn't Get His Wish

In a small town in northern Mississippi in 1946, an eleven-year-old boy begged his parents, once again, for a bicycle. It cost too much, his parents told him, way too much; but he was their only child, and his mother wanted to give him something special. She thought and thought about what else he might like that she and his daddy could afford.

Finally she found something at the Tupelo Hardware Company. It cost $12.95.

The boy accepted the gift, a guitar, and he learned how to play it. He played and sang so well that when they moved to Memphis in 1948, he began spending a lot of time on Beale Street, learning the blues and picking gospel tunes. In 1953, wanting to hear what his recorded voice sounded like, he

Elvis Presley, shown here at age ten, had to settle for a guitar as a birthday gift because his parents couldn't afford a bicycle. (COURTESY GRACELAND)

dropped into Sun Records' Memphis Recording Service and made a demo for his mother, singing "My Happiness" and "That's When Your Heartaches Begin."

You know the rest of this boy's story. Now you know that if his parents had been able to afford a bicycle instead of a guitar, we might never have heard of Elvis Presley.

What Started Out as the "Grand Alt(ernative) Opry"

The house band is named Vacation Bible School and is billed as "the most righteous band in the land." Now known as Billy Block's Western Beat, the show was started by Block as a way to bring back a love of country and alternative music to Nashville. The Cinderella-type story began in 1995, when Billy Block came to Tennessee from California, where he had been the house drummer at the famous Hollywood honky-tonk, the Palomino Club. He started his show, first billed as the "Grand Alt Opry," on a shoestring and a prayer. Within months his Tuesday-night live concert series and radio show at a small south Nashville bar outgrew its setting and moved twice to accommodate larger audiences. It's now located at a club called the Exit/In.

Block's Western Beat idea, with its frequent switching of musicians who perform with the Vacation Bible School, was an instant hit. Since its inception, Western Beat has showcased more than six hundred artists, including Steve Earle, Lucinda Williams, Leroy Parnell, the Derailers, Marty Stuart, and Trisha Yearwood, with some of them appearing on a Country Music Television (CMT) weekly series that debuted Block's show in July 2000.

Embracing the newest technology, Western Beat is also aired every Tuesday night via the Internet (Live on the Net at www.westernbeat.com), which reaches a potential audience of at least seventy million listeners and viewers. This way, if you can't walk in, log on.

 MUSIC TRIVIA I

Q. What Bristol-born entertainer, known for the song "Sixteen Tons," closed his TV shows with the signature line, "Bless your little pea-picking hearts"?

A. Tennessee Ernie Ford.

Q. What Jackson native wrote the hit song "Blue Suede Shoes"?

A. Carl Perkins.

Q. In 1967, the Country Music Association's first Entertainer of the Year award went to what country music singer?

A. Eddy Arnold.

Q. With their headquarters in Hendersonville, what group of contemporary country-pop groups released such well-known songs as "Sail Away" and "Elvira"?

A. The Oak Ridge Boys.

Q. When President Richard M. Nixon visited the Grand Ole Opry in 1974, what Opry star gave him yo-yo lessons?

A. Roy Acuff.

Q. James D. Vaughn transformed what city into the "capital of gospel music in America"?

A. Lawrenceburg.

Q. In the 1980 TV special *Hank Williams: The Man and His Music,* actor Henry Arnold played the part of what Nashville-based music publisher?

A. Fred Rose.

Q. What country music star was a heavyweight boxer in the Washington, D.C., area before making it in country music?

A. Roy Clark.

Q. In what Tennessee town did Elvis play his last concert as a warm-up act?

A. Kingsport in 1955. (He preceded the Louvin Brothers and Cowboy Copas, for which he was paid around thirty-seven dollars.)

Q. What country music star, who made her acting debut in the science-fiction movie *Tremors,* also starred as fictional race-car star A. J. Ferguson in the 1994 version of *The Little Rascals?*

A. Reba McEntire.

Q. The spiritual "They That Sow in Tears Shall Reap in Joy," which premiered in 1955 at Overton Park in Memphis, was written by what composer who died in 1958?

A. W. C. Handy.

Q. In what year was Sun Records bought by Shelby Singleton?

A. 1969.

Q. From 1954 to 1956, who was Hank Snow's manager?

A. Colonel Tom Parker.

Q. When he appeared on *The Louisiana Hayride* in the 1950s, who called himself "the Singing Fisherman"?

A. Johnny Horton.

Q. What famous RCA studio in Nashville was built in 1957, at the insistence of Chet Atkins?

A. Studio B.

Q. What tune was played when Governor Frank Clement went to the podium to make the keynote address at the 1956 Democratic National Convention?

A. "The Tennessee Waltz."

Q. What was the first publication for country music and musicians to be published in the United States?

A. *Country Music Roundup.*

Q. Where is Elvis Presley's 1960 "Solid Gold Cadillac"?

A. Country Music Hall of Fame and Museum.

Q. Who was the first woman to be named Entertainer of the Year by the Country Music Association?

A. Loretta Lynn, in 1972.

Q. What name was given to musicians Willie Nelson, Waylon Jennings, Jessie Colter, and Tompall Glaser (and band), who found fame in Nashville?

A. The Outlaws.

Twice in a Lifetime:
The Comeback Queen of Blues and Jazz

When the eighty-two-year-old black singer arrived on stage in 1979 at the Cookery, a New York nightclub, the sensation of appearing before an audience was one she hadn't felt in more than twenty years. The songs she sang that night, from "My Castle's Rockin'" to "Down-Hearted Blues," echoed her life from her early days in Memphis where she grew up to where she now stood, at the beginning of her comeback. This woman was Alberta Hunter, one of America's legendary singers of blues and jazz.

Her life was successful against improbable odds. Her mother worked in a Memphis brothel as a maid, and Hunter began singing there, performing tunes she'd heard on Beale Street.

Hunter's throaty voice made her a star from the 1920s through the mid-1950s; she had toured with the first all-black USO troupe to entertain troops at the front in World War II and the Korean War.

Abruptly quitting show-biz and becoming a nurse when her mother died, she worked at a Manhattan hospital until she was eighty-two.

That's when her career took off. Again.

Barney Josephson, the owner of the Cookery, heard that Hunter was living as a retired nurse in New York. He called and told her, "Get on down here. You're going to be a singer again." Someone who heard her remembers: "She had an incredible presence. She had our attention . . . and even at eighty-two, she was sexy!"

Alberta Hunter performed at the Cookery until her death in 1986, a star twice in her lifetime.

Guess Who? He grew up in Union County outside Maynardsville and his dream was to play professional baseball. Earning twelve letters in high school, he had good prospects to realize his dream. Then he was invited to try out for the New York Yankees, but the young man first went to Florida, where he acquired a terrible sunburn.

It was so severe he required hospitalization and a year of bed rest. Recuperating from his burns, his pro-ball dreams shattered, the young man began to listen to the Grand Ole Opry, and he decided to try to play the kind of music he heard. His first appearance on the Opry was in 1938.

Who is he? Roy Acuff, now known as one of the kings of country music.

An Impromptu Concert Series

In the summer of 1962 a young man first came into Collins Music Store in Clarksville. He introduced himself to the owner, Sam Collins, saying he

was stationed nearby at Fort Campbell and would like to drop in from time to time. Collins got to know the young man and remembered him later as someone who talked fast yet not discourteously. "He'd come in here and pick up any guitar and just start playing it," he recently recalled. "He liked to play rock and roll . . . and I knew he had a sound I didn't hear every day. And he had a set of lungs that could really belt out the songs."

During the early 1960s Jimi Hendrix gave impromptu performances at Collins Music Store in Clarksville. (COURTESY COLLINS MUSIC STORE)

Collins and others who were in the music store when the young man came by now consider themselves lucky to have heard those impromptu concerts. The young man was none other than the legendary Jimi Hendrix.

Cinderella Story: One Coal Miner's Daughter

Born in 1935 in Kentucky coal mining country, Loretta Lynn sang about as soon as she spoke her first words, and when the Grand Ole Opry came on the radio each Saturday night, she'd be found glued to the speaker, absorbing every note. Married at the age of thirteen, she went from coal miner's daughter to coal miner's wife.

After seeing so many of his friends and family die young, their lungs choked by coal dust, her husband, "Mooney," left coal mining soon after their marriage and they moved to Washington State. Music was still in Loretta's veins, though, so Mooney encouraged her to try singing professionally. By 1950 she had started performing at area honky-tonks, and by the 1960s she'd performed on Buck Owens's radio show out of Tacoma and had released her first single, which she wrote herself, "I'm a Honky Tonk Girl."

With her husband as manager, Loretta achieved success in her singing career, with appearances on Ernest Tubb's *Midnight Jamboree* on WSM Radio and an invitation to become a regular on the Grand Ole Opry. Her closest friend was Patsy Cline, who influenced her singing style. The coal miner's daughter became one of Tennessee's diamonds when she and her husband made their home in Nashville and then at Hurricane Mills in Humphreys County.

It is the story in her songs that makes people love Loretta Lynn. Her audiences share the experiences of the girl who grew up in oppressive poverty and a life of back-breaking work, but with dreams about which she sings. Her story has been such an inspiration that her book *Coal Miner's Daughter* (1976) was made into a blockbuster movie starring Sissy Spacek as Loretta Lynn and Tommy Lee Jones as Mooney.

The Country Music Hall of Fame

Located in Nashville, the Country Music Hall of Fame was originally founded in 1961 by the Country Music Association (CMA), but is now its own entity. The first inductees were Jimmie Rodgers, Fred Rose, and Hank Williams Sr., that same year. Inductees are chosen every year by an anonymous panel of two hundred people who have actively participated in the music business for fifteen years or more and who themselves have made a significant contribution to the music industry.

The Country Music Hall of Fame and Museum has been visited by over ten million people, making it one of the most visited musical museums in the country. It includes over three thousand items relating to the people and history of country music. The media center contains over two hundred thousand recorded discs, sixty thousand photographs, five thousand films and videotapes, posters, songbooks, and hundreds of audiotapes.

Important to country music and its history is what the museum does in

Fans meet Country Music Hall of Fame member Eddy Arnold at the museum. (COURTESY COUNTRY MUSIC HALL OF FAME, NASHVILLE, TENN.)

the fields of restoration and education. It restores priceless historical commercial recordings and each year helps over twenty thousand students and teachers with lesson plans, classroom materials, and other musical educational aids. A mentoring program for promising young songwriters and a Girl Scout program called Camp SummerSong engender a love of country music and music in general. All this has given country music a new, more sophisticated image.

Country Music: So They Say

★ "A song ain't nothin' in the world but a story just wrote with music to it."—Hank Williams Sr.

★ "Country music springs from the heart of America."—Tex Ritter

★ "A good country song taps into strong undercurrents of family, faith, and patriotism."—George Bush Sr.

★ "When you stop dreaming, you stop living."—Lorrie Morgan

★ "Keep learning, keep doing, and get your ducks in a row. Then, when opportunity knocks, you're ready."—Buck Owens

★ "True country music is honesty, sincerity, and real life to the hilt." —Garth Brooks

★ "If you want the rainbow, you've got to put up with a little rain." —Dolly Parton

★ "As an artist, it tells me we are doing our job when we're touching people's hearts."—Ty Herndon

★ "God respects you when you work, but he loves you when you sing."—Cliffie Stone

★ "Applause surely must be the most powerful aphrodisiac known to mankind. The quest for it is a disease of the blood. Or, at best, a genetic disorder."— "Whisperin' Bill" Anderson

★ "I started in rock and worked my way up to country."—Conway Twitty

She's Got L'eggs

Born in the West Tennessee town of Nutbush of sharecropper parents, Anna Mae Bullock picked cotton and did all the other necessary backbreaking work in a hardscrabble farm family. As she grew, she began to listen to WDIA, the black radio station in Memphis, where she heard the music of blues greats such as Sleepy John Estes, Bootsie Whitelow, and B. B. King. Moving to St. Louis with her mother, she became female singer of a band, the Kings of Rhythm. She and the bandleader married, and they became the most famous husband-and-wife act in R&B and, later, rock music; however, their marriage ended because he was abusive.

Now she is perhaps one of the highest achievers in musical entertainment.

She has written her autobiography, and although she was born in 1939, she still has such great legs that she's the spokesperson for L'eggs pantyhose.

You know her as Tina Turner; her husband was Ike Turner.

It Started with a KISS

This country music singer, who moved to Nashville in 1984, recalled the time he thought he was getting his first big break: "One night around six o'clock," he related to interviewer Ralph Emery, "we got a call from a promoter asking us if we could put a band together and get down to the [Norman, Oklahoma] civic center by eight o'clock." When he saw the marquee announcing that the rock band KISS was playing that night, the would-be star was incredulous and thought he couldn't be opening for that particular group.

But he was! Bravely, he and his hastily put together band played their part as the warm-up band. The audience was unappreciative to say the least. The band was booed off the stage by people who had come expecting to hear rock music.

That was the school-of-hard-knocks beginning of the country star you know as Vince Gill.

Tennessee Singer Takes a Bite Out of "the Big Apple"

We were in the labor and delivery unit of Nashville's Baptist Hospital in 1990, getting ready to have our first baby. But the nurses and staff seemed to have their minds elsewhere. Finally I asked, "What's going on?"

"Garth Brooks and his wife, Sandy, are down the hall," they said. "They're having their first baby."

That was the closest I've ever gotten to the star whose lyrics, showmanship, and singing style have endeared him to country music fans and who has made fans out of people who weren't country music fans. Some of Brooks's biographers say he's the biggest-selling solo artist in U.S. music history.

One reason he's done so well is that he's in it for the music. Instead of thinking of studio schedules and other time-restrictive considerations, Brooks plays the recordings until they sound right, experimenting with different approaches and various instruments until the sound in his imagination and the sound in his ears are the same.

Nashville's hard on a musician's heart, though. When Brooks first came to Music City and his dreams weren't realized right away, he nearly left to go back to Oklahoma and the girl he'd left behind. Calling Sandy one night, he said simply, "It's not for me. I'm on my way home." Maybe something she said that night encouraged him, for Garth stuck with his dream, married Sandy, and then his career took off.

Brooks even has enough energy and enthusiasm to excite Tennessee's more northerly neighbors in New York City. His concert in Central Park on August 7, 1997, drew a record-breaking crowd.

His heart's as big as Tennessee is wide. He recently lived a dream of his own, training with the San Diego baseball team, the Padres, in spring 1999 and donating all his earnings to his charity for children, Touch 'Em All.

I haven't met him yet, but maybe when I do, we'll compare baby pictures.

Did You Know? As a young man, Mel Tillis couldn't keep a job because of his terrible stutter. He'd been a fireman, a strawberry picker, and a house painter. When he applied to be a driver of a candy-company truck, the employer wouldn't hire him but gave him a copy of the Serenity Prayer, which asks for wisdom to "accept the things I cannot change." The young man began to write songs, which he could sing without stuttering. He started out as a backup musician and songwriter, and he's now a famous country music singer.

Records Setting Records!

Here are some record-breaking entries from the 1999 *Guinness Book of World Records*:

★ Garth Brooks became the most successful country music recording artist, selling more than $80 million worth of albums between 1989 and 1998.

★ The late Tammy Wynette, who was often called the "First Lady of Country Music," was the first female country music singer to sell a million records in 1969.

★ The late Conway Twitty had the most songs make the number-one spot on the country charts, with forty tunes on the *Billboard* hit list.

 ## MUSIC TRIVIA II

Q. What classical music label made Franklin its world headquarters in 1999?
A. NAXOS.

Q. What name was given to the Grand Ole Opry's show that performed for American soldiers at home and overseas during World War II?
A. Camel Caravan.

Q. In 1871 spirituals were introduced to other parts of the country by what group of black singers?
A. The Jubilee Singers, of Fisk University, Nashville.

Q. A 1963 plane crash near Camden killed what four musicians?
A. Patsy Cline, Cowboy Copas, Randy Hughes, and Hawkshaw Hawkins.

Q. With what well-known Memphis personality did Isaac Hayes open a branch of the L. Ron Hubbard's School of Scientology in Memphis in 1997?
A. Lisa Marie Presley, daughter of the late Elvis Presley.

Q. The Country Music Awards were first broadcast on network TV in what year?

A. 1968.

Q. Who coined the term "country music"?

A. Connie B. Gay.

Q. What country music celebrity interviewer wrote three books of memoirs entitled *Memories, More Memories,* and *The View from Nashville?*

A. Ralph Emery.

Q. After leaving the Opry, what singer/songwriter moved to Missouri, where he was host of one of the first successful country television programs, *Ozark Jubilee?*

A. Clyde Julian "Red" Foley (1910–1968).

Q. What man, known as the world's lowest bass singer, performed with the Blackwood Brothers and the Sunshine Boys, and toured with Elvis Presley?

A. J. D. Sumner.

Q. What popular Memphis entertainer, who blends his music with Cajun, bluegrass, and jazz, is known as "Gatemouth"?

A. Clarence Brown.

Q. What grandfatherly type on the syndicated country TV show *Hee Haw* loved to belt out the song "Old Rattler"?

A. Grandpa Jones.

Q. On what nationally televised show did Elvis Presley first appear?

A. *The Ed Sullivan Show,* in 1956.

Q. What 1962 hit song by Lester Flatt of Flatt and Scruggs became the song for a popular TV show about some mountain people who discovered oil and suddenly became rich?

A. "The Ballad of Jed Clampett."

Q. "You Light Up My Life" was the hit song for what daughter of Pat Boone?

A. Debby Boone.

Q. What U.S. president said he favored country music above all other kinds of music?

A. George Bush Sr. (His favorite artist is Roy Acuff.)

Q. What group did Hendersonville resident Roy Orbison open for in England in 1963?

A. The Beatles. (They later wrote "Please Please Me" for him.)

Q. After he filled in for Hank Williams in 1952, what singer was immediately offered a contract with the show *Louisiana Hayride?*

A. Jim Reeves, who joined the Grand Ole Opry in 1955.

Q. Known as the "singing cowboy," what Grand Ole Opry star was also a stock-car racer?

A. Marty Robbins.

Q. What musician, with his "galloping guitar" method of picking, was the youngest member of the Country Music Hall of Fame when he was inducted in 1973?

A. Chet Atkins.

Deana Carter

"In our family you either had to sing harmony or wash dishes," Deana Carter quips. "So naturally I picked the harmony part."

Her father, Fred Carter Jr., played on virtually all the recording sessions in Nashville during the 1960s and 1970s, with such greats as Roy Orbison, Simon and Garfunkel, and Elvis Presley. Deana Carter's own first break came when Willie Nelson heard one of her demo tapes and asked her to perform in a Farm Aid concert.

She was the only female soloist in the show, but made friends with the crowd and became an overnight sensation, recording such hits as "Did I Shave My Legs for This?" and "Strawberry Wine."

All the times she sang to get out of washing dishes finally paid off.

Unusual Country Music Song Titles

★ "There's a Tear in My Beer"—Hank Williams Jr. and Hank Williams Sr.

★ "I Ain't No Communist"—Grandpa Jones

★ "Truck-Crashin' Cousin"—Curtis Danny Glen

★ "Achy-Breaky Heart"—Billy Ray Cyrus

★ "White Trash Shine My Shoes"—Mark Gilman and Jay Smith

★ "A Truck Called Sunday School"—Don Schauda

★ "Truck Accordion"—Jonathan DeWitt Sampson

★ "Did I Shave My Legs for This?"—Deana Carter

★ "Did I Shave My Back for This?"—Cletus Judd (in response to Carter's song)

★ "She Ran Out of Give Before I Ran Out of Take"—Phil Lee

★ "Cheatin' Ain't Cheatin' When Nobody Knows"—Thomas Allen and Larry Lee

★ "Barroom Bathroom Stall"—Steven Tracy

★ "Scarlet O'Hara Is Alive and Well"—Mike Rayburn

Strange . . . but True

How Tootsie Kept Order in Her Lounge

In March 1960, Hattie Louise "Tootsie" Bess bought a lounge in Nashville near the Ryman Auditorium, then the home of the Grand Ole Opry. Tootsie's Orchid Lounge was essentially a place for Opry performers and down-on-their-luck musicians to come, take their breaks, and have some of Tootsie's fried chicken and beer. Some of her regulars included Roger Miller, Willie Nelson, Kris Kristofferson, Tom T. Hall, and Loretta Lynn ("she usually came in to get Mooney," one long-time patron said).

How did Tootsie keep her patrons from getting too rambunctious? She didn't use a pistol to keep the peace, or even a burly bouncer. She used the time-honored lady's tool: a hat pin. Whoever acted up got stuck!

Although it's now under new ownership, proprietor Steve Smith still uses the hat pin. "Everybody here stays in line," he said.

"Pretty Women Don't Need Money"

One day Roy Orbison's wife, Claudette, was about to go out shopping. He'd written a song for her and was discussing just what to name it with his friend Bill Dees. As Claudette was leaving, Roy asked her if she needed money.

Dees looked at Roy and quipped, "Don't you know that pretty women don't need money?" Orbison and Dees looked at each other and said in unison, "Pretty Woman!" It was the perfect title for Orbison's song, which has enjoyed enduring popularity and was used as the title song for the movie *Pretty Woman*, starring Julia Roberts and Richard Gere.

Good thing Claudette decided to go shopping that day.

Guess Who? This man was born in Covington in 1942, the son of a sharecropper. He was raised by his grandparents in Memphis, where he learned to play the saxophone and piano. In 1962 his first band, Sir Isaac and the DooDads, did gigs at local clubs. By 1964 he was playing backup on the keyboard for Otis Redding, Carla Thomas, and others at Stax Recording Studio. His shaved head in the time when afros were popular made him stand out. He was, and is, a symbol of black pride and success, the first African American composer to win an Academy Award. The voice of Chef on the animated TV show *South Park* belongs to this man.

Who is he? Isaac Hayes, whose "Theme for Shaft" won him that Academy Award.

A Job from Chet Atkins

The following story was told by Muriel Anderson, internationally renowned guitar player, who was lucky enough to have Chet Atkins as a mentor.

"Like many young guitarists, I often stopped by Chet Atkins's office in Nashville with the hopes he might be practicing a tune, and I could learn some music by watching his fingers. Chet was always very generous with his music, and sometimes he would slow it down so that I could catch the notes as they went by. I learned a lot of music this way.

"One day as I was talking to his secretary, Mr. Atkins came down the stairs and said, 'Muriel, I have a job for you!' The greatest guitarist in the world giving *me* a job? What could it be, the Grand Ole Opry? Carnegie Hall?

"'You see,' he continued, 'my pet rooster, Hot Shot, has come down with a case of feather mites, and my wife and I are getting too old to crawl into the chicken coop, and we're just too big, and . . . you see, you're about the smallest person I know.' He went on to tell me that he was going to ask [Grand Ole Opry star] Little Jimmy Dickens, but I just happened into the office that day.

"That afternoon I went to the Atkinses' home. They put a plastic bag with head- and armholes over me to protect my clothes, and with a great deal of coaching, I caught the rooster by both legs at once (so the spurs didn't get me) and with the other hand grabbed its neck. Then Chet's wife, Leona, spread bacon grease around its neck for the mite dust to adhere to. Then I caught the hen (also named Leona) and we covered her with mite dust as well, while the rooster complained loudly.

"With that, Mrs. Atkins put a little more water in the stew, and I was invited to stay for lunch. Chicken stew, I believe it was."

Chet Atkins gives Muriel Anderson a guitar lesson. He also gave her a job helping out in his chicken coop. (COURTESY MURIEL ANDERSON)

The Story of Sleepy John Estes

Born in Brownsville, guitar player John Estes earned his nickname, "Sleepy," because he could drop off for a nap at a moment's notice. After recording in Chicago for a few years with both the Bluebird and Decca record labels, he returned to West Tennessee. Estes was recording at Sun Studio in Memphis in the early 1950s when tragedy struck. Sleepy John's vision started to fail (his sight was already impaired from a childhood eye trauma). As his vision diminished, his despair intensified, and the notes issued less frequently from his guitar. Once he was completely blind, he dropped out of the music scene and returned to Brownsville to live out his life in obscurity.

But the blues were rediscovered in the 1960s, and along with them, Sleepy John Estes. He was brought from his shack in Brownsville back into the music scene. He picked up where he left off and from then on recorded and toured internationally until his death in 1977. Now the town that calls itself the "heart of the Tennessee Delta" has created a museum in honor of its own "Delta blues man," Sleepy John Estes.

The Legendary Brenda Lee

Here are some tidbits from Ralph Emery, music celebrity interviewer, about rock and country legend Brenda Lee, who began singing in Nashville in 1956.

★ She's sold more double-sided hit singles than any other female in pop music's history.

★ She's charted in more categories more consistently than any other female in recording history.

★ During the 1960s Lee was the top female act and fourth overall (the top three being Elvis Presley, the Beatles, and Ray Charles).

★ She's ranked number nine for most consecutive top ten hits of all time.

★ Her first hit song in the United States was the 1960s release, "Sweet Nothings."

Did You Know? The only person with four relatives in the Country Music Hall of Fame is June Carter Cash. She has an aunt (Sara Carter), an uncle (A. P. Carter), her mother (Mother Maybelle Carter), and her husband (Johnny Cash) honored there.

Bessie Smith: "Hold It!"

Chattanooga-born Bessie Smith (1894–1937) is said to be the "Empress of the Blues." The songs she made famous, such as "Jail-House Blues" and Alberta Hunter's "Down Hearted Blues" left music fans enthralled. She was raised by her sister in a one-room wooden shack in a poor neighborhood in Chattanooga called Blue Goose Hollow. She and her brother Clarence were street musicians by the time she was nine, with Bessie singing and Clarence accompanying her on his guitar.

The renowned blues singer Gertrude "Ma" Rainey took her on as a pupil, and Frank Walker, head of Columbia Records' Race Division, had her come for an audition on February 15, 1923.

Two weeks before the Columbia audition, Smith had "blown it" at a New York audition. She had been invited to audition at Okeh Records in New York. She cut a test song, then interrupted the audition with, "Hold it! I gotta spit!" That was the end of that audition; the studio personnel said she was "too rough" for audiences.

When Smith auditioned for Columbia, apparently she didn't spit, because they asked her back the following day. On that day she sang songs that would comprise her first release as a professional blues singer: "Gulf Coast Blues" and "Down Hearted Blues." Bessie Smith was on her way.

Two "Cash" Coincidences

In 1987 when Rosanne Cash recorded "Tennessee Flat-Top Box," she thought the song was in the public domain. Until it debuted on the *Billboard* charts and reached the number one spot, she was still unaware that her father, Johnny Cash, had written and recorded it in 1962.

Twelve years later, in Hendersonville, June Carter Cash sat singing "Ring of Fire," one of Johnny Cash's hit songs. At sixty-nine years of age, she had just released a CD *(Press On)*, which included that song. She sang it as if she'd written every word, and she had, many years earlier, in the midst of the sweet anguish of new love.

That love interest was Johnny Cash. "I realized I had fallen in love with Johnny Cash," she said. "It was not an opportune time for this to happen and I wouldn't have told him and I just hoped he'd never find it out." They were both married to other people, and for years he didn't know what feelings had prompted her to write those lyrics. Years later, the secret came out and they married.

Now the new rendition of the song Johnny Cash sang back then has been recorded by the person who really wrote it.

She Couldn't Act, but . . .

Twenty-eight-year-old Sarah Ophelia Cannon just couldn't make it in acting and had gone back home to Centerville, frustrated, to get a job as a recreation-room director. One night the children in her program entertained at a bankers' convention. While waiting for the main speaker to arrive, Ophelia filled in with her monologue about a fictitious girl from the fictitious mountain village called Grinder's Switch.

That did it. She went on to become a star of the Grand Ole Opry—named Minnie Pearl.

Some Pearls from Minnie

Here are some samples of Minnie Pearl's humor from *The Best Jokes Minnie Pearl Ever Told,* compiled by Kevin Kenworthy (Nashville: Rutledge Hill Press, 1999):

> This afternoon when I left Grinder's Switch down there where I live at, my friend Lizzy Tinkem said, "Oh, I sure do envy you goin' up to the Grand Ole Opry every Saturday night where all them handsome fellers are. Now if you see some really handsome fellers up there tonight, you flirt with 'em just for me, hear?"
>
> So when I got to the Opry I saw Grant Turner. So I flirted a little with Grant. I did it for Lizzy, of course, not for me. Then I saw old Ernie Newton, and I kinda flirted with him for Lizzy, not for me. But when I seen that Rex Allen, that's when I decided to go into business for myself!

> A young mother enlisted the help of a friend in taking her identical infant twins to the doctor. Since the waiting area was full, the two women, each with a twin, were seated on opposite sides of the room. After a few minutes someone who came in later commented, "It's amazing how much your two babies look alike." The friend was quick to reply, saying, "Well, they should. They have the same father!"

MUSIC TRIVIA III

Q. What banjo-playing star of *Hee-Haw* and the Grand Ole Opry was tragically murdered in his home in Goodlettsville in the 1960s?

A. David Akeman, nicknamed "Stringbean."

Q. What do the call letters WSM stand for in the radio station that has always broadcast the Opry from Nashville?

A. "We Shield Millions," the motto of National Life and Accident Insurance Company, which originally owned the station.

Q. What was the "chitlin circuit," and how did it relate to the blues?

A. Blues nightclubs would serve chitlins as a side dish to their dinners. Traveling blues players denoted their "circuit" this way.

Q. What Memphis radio station in the 1950s was the first dedicated to black music?

A. WDIA, home of Rufus Thomas, the famous DJ whose own hits include "Walking the Dog."

Q. What blues musician called Beale Street "a city unto itself" in his autobiography?

A. B. B. King.

Q. Astronaut Pete Conrad took along the tapes of what musician on the *Apollo 12* mission?

A. Faron Young, who was posthumously inducted into the Country Music Hall of Fame in June 2000.

Q. Virginia Patterson Hensley won the Arthur Godfrey talent contest in 1957 for singing what song?

A. "Walking after Midnight." (Patsy Cline was her stage name.)

Q. What was the day job of Walter "Furry" Lewis, who played the blues by night with W. C. Handy, had a movie role in *W.W. and the Dixie Dance Kings*, and toured the United States and Europe with the Memphis Blues Caravan?

A. Street cleaner for the city of Memphis.

Q. What Memphis native, Rock and Roll Hall of Fame inductee, and Grammy winner was sued for breach of contract in 1984 for not singing in the Broadway musical *Sing, Mahalia, Sing*?

A. Aretha Franklin, who didn't appear because she was afraid of flying.

Q. What is Nashville saxophone player Boots Randolph's best-known tune?

A. "Yakety Sax."

Q. Uncle Dave Macon of the Grand Ole Opry had what nickname?

A. "Dixie Dewdrop."

Q. Other than the Museum of Appalachia house band, what was the only Caucasian group to perform at the memorial service of *Roots* author Alex Haley?

A. The Foster Family Band, led by Dr. William Foster, who was born in Soddy-Daisy.

Q. Musicians Ernest Ferguson (mandolin player), Howdy Forrester, and Paul Warren (both fiddlers) all claim what county as home?

A. Hickman.

Q. Brentwood resident Mary Frances Penick uses what stage name?

A. Skeeter Davis.

Q. What annual national music award is named after a Memphis musician?

A. W. C. Handy Blues Musician of the Year.

Q. Around 1903 what gospel songwriter organized some Beale Street musicians and called them the Music Club?

A. Lucie Campbell.

Q. What country musician made a cameo appearance in the 1999 kids' movie *Baby Geniuses*?

A. Randy Travis had one line, as a control technician in the amusement-park scene.

Q. In 1903, when Chattanooga-born Bessie Smith made one of her first performances in a theater in her hometown at the age of nine, how much was she paid?

A. Eight dollars.

Q. What is the longest running syndicated country comedy TV show?

A. *Hee Haw.*

Q. Country Music Hall of Fame member Hank Williams had what congenital deformity?

A. A defect of the lower spine that caused him to stand with a stoop.

11

Flora, Fauna, and
Natural Phenomena

Tennessee Walking Horses

Tennesseans, with their neighbors from all over the world, get together for ten days every summer in Shelbyville, for what is now called simply "the Celebration," a festival and competition featuring the famed Tennessee Walking Horse.

Originally bred for long rides around the plantation, these horses were called a lot of different names, including "all purpose horse" and "southern plantation saddle horse." As breeders in Middle Tennessee came to have a reputation for raising horses with a smooth, even gait, buyers came from outside the area wanting to buy "those walking horses," and that was the name that stuck. If it's a good walker, the horse has a disposition as easy as it's ride.

The Tennessee walking horse became a recognized breed in 1935, when the Tennessee Walking Horse Breeders' Association was organized in Lewisburg. From that time on, this special breed of horse has enjoyed an incredible popularity, as has the Celebration. The original Tennessee Walking Horse was F Allen One. Another famous stud, Strolling Jim, was trained by his owner, Floyd Carothers, on the grounds of the hotel now called the Walking Horse Hotel in Wartrace.

In the 1939 competition, Strolling Jim was named the first Tennessee

189

Walking Horse World Grand Champion. Wartrace then became known as "the Cradle of the Tennessee Walking Horse." Strolling Jim is buried behind the old hotel, but folks around there say they sometimes see his ghost strolling the grounds as he did in the old days.

Mule Day in Columbia

Since the 1930s, if you were in the market to buy a mule, you'd come to the town of Columbia to look for one. What started with some mules and their traders gathering to meet with prospective buyers has become known as Mule Day, now the world's largest mule market.

Mule Day is a regular event held every April, complete with music, dancing, and a big parade. (Mule Day 2000 was celebrated as "the Mule-Lennium.") But who really buys mules nowadays? Well, the Amish for one. And ever ride a mule down into the Grand Canyon? Those mules are bred in Tennessee. Good mules don't come cheap. A proper pair of mules might lighten your wallet by around six or seven thousand dollars.

Puts mules in a whole other light, doesn't it? Maybe next time you pass a mule, you'll tip your hat.

Kinda Like a Beauty Contest: The Rules for Mules

Curious as to exactly how mules are judged, I located a man by the name of Jerry Erwin, who is cochairman of the Mule Day event. Here's what he said:

"It's kinda like a beauty contest. I mean, if you're judging a mule, you want the best-looking one. They must have long ears erected on the corners of the head. The face must have little fat under the jaw-bone. They must have a thin neck, wide chest, and a straight back. Their body must have graceful lines, and the back legs must be only slightly bowed.

"Their hooves should be medium-sized, not too big or small. No pigeon-toes. No knock-knees. They should be a big-boned animal with good muscle tone and development. They should have a nice walk and carry themselves well."

He almost made me break out in song—something like, "There she is . . ."

> *Did You Know?* Shelby County has more horses per capita than any other county in the United States.

Reelfoot Lake: Earthquake City, Land of Eagles

In northwestern Tennessee, where Missouri, Kentucky, and Tennessee borders meet, there is a place unlike any other. Visiting Reelfoot Lake is like being on another planet or going back in time, when Earth was ruled more by animals than by humankind. Its topography gives it a sense of the surreal.

Reelfoot Lake is situated on the New Madrid fault, and back in the winter of 1811–12 huge earthquakes occurred there. Violence was such that a fissure opened between the Mississippi River and the Cypress Bottoms of the lake area. Archeologists have said that for three days the Mississippi River flowed backward, filling the bottoms and creating Reelfoot, the only large natural lake in Tennessee.

Bald eagles nest in the cypress swamps of Reelfoot Lake. (COURTESY DAVID HAGGARD)

The cypress trees still stand, their wide wooden "knees" just above water level. Reelfoot has a lot of the fauna you might see in the rest of this part of the country: egrets, loons, ospreys, cormorants, and blue herons. You'll see evidence of quails, deer, doves, and turkeys—and if you're quiet enough, you might even spot them. The forests around the lake abound with raccoons, rabbits, and squirrels, and there have been more than fifty-six different species of fish caught in the lake.

From October through the end of March, Reelfoot is the busiest. Ducks, not by the thousands, but by the hundreds of thousands, come to Reelfoot to winter. The mallard population alone has surpassed four hundred thousand, with nearly one hundred thousand Canada geese.

When you think of Tennessee, do you think of bald eagles? Probably not, but Reelfoot Lake is one of their winter homes and nesting areas, and you can take guided tours to see their aeries—incredible nests of twigs and sticks that average six feet across.

When you see it for yourself, you'll understand why this area was the favorite hunting ground of David Crockett and Jim Bowie.

Strange . . . but True

What in the Sandhill?

Every February the people of the Birchwood community (about thirty miles northeast of Chattanooga) hold the Sandhill Crane Festival to celebrate the more than thirty-five thousand sandhill cranes that use the nearby Hiwassee Wildlife Refuge to rest from their migrations. The cranes arrive from southern Canada and the Great Lakes region every October to winter in northern Florida or southern Georgia, but more and more of them have been choosing to remain in Tennessee. In the middle of the 1998–99 winter, for example, there were more than five thousand sandhill cranes staying in the Hiwassee Wildlife Refuge. The last ones leave by the latter part of March each year.

Hohenwald's Elephants

In the tiny hamlet of Hohenwald, people who live a few miles outside the town are awakened every morning, not to birdsong, nor to rooster crow, but to elephant trumpeting. Hohenwald is the host to the Elephant Sanctuary, the "first natural environment for elephants in the United States," according to its codirectors, Carol Buckley and Scott Blais.

When circuses, zoos, and other entertainment-oriented businesses had no further use for old elephants, there was no place for them to go. And when elephants are no longer capable of performing, their upkeep becomes too expensive. Elephants eat around 150 pounds of hay and grain daily, at an annual cost of around twelve thousand dollars. Thus many elephants, especially Asian ones, were neglected—even starving.

Enter Buckley and Blais. Recognizing that Hohenwald's environment is similar to Asia's, they decided to settle their sanctuary in that part of Tennessee. Their first elephant arrived in 1995. True to the meaning of the term *sanctuary,* no tourists are allowed, although you can see the elephants via teleconferencing or accessing their website.

Residents of the Elephant Sanctuary in Hohenwald enjoy a light snack of watermelons.
(COURTESY OF THE ELEPHANT SANCTUARY IN HOHENWALD)

Here the pachyderms are free to graze, wander the 112-acre sanctuary—and paint. "With more than one hundred thousand muscles in their trunks," Buckley explained, "they're very adept at picking up small things or wielding a paintbrush." Their best artist is Tarra, and I have a "signed" original.

Tiger, Tiger . . .

On forty-seven acres outside Kingsport in East Tennessee, the residents do the kinds of things you might expect on a farm, like go out and feed the livestock. But in this case the "stock" isn't cows, pigs, and chickens. Here the stock is fed twelve hundred pounds of red meat. This is a sanctuary known as Tiger Haven, a safe place for unwanted tigers, leopards, lions, and other big animals in the feline family, one of only about five in the United States.

Tiger Haven was established in 1991 for big cats who have been abused and mistreated, and it has grown to include more than sixty-three such animals. Despite anxiety from nervous neighbors, there have never been any escapes from Tiger Haven.

Where do these unwanted cats come from? A problem occurs when regular folks buy the cats, thinking they would make a "different" kind of pet. Well, they are different, but they are not meant to be pets. Owner Joe Parker says, "When people see big cats perform on TV and in circuses, it creates a desire to possess such beauty and power while leading us to believe we can contain and control the power and emotions of a great cat." With most states having no laws regulating the commerce and keeping of cats, the regular folks who wanted to raise a giant, lovable "Tigger" for their kids suddenly find themselves broke from feeding the cat and fearing for their lives. Even if a big cat means no harm, playing with a heavy animal with sharp claws and teeth can end in disaster.

Zoos don't take these unwanted animals because of their licensing requirements—no stray cats allowed. So what happens to a big cat when it's no longer wanted or needed by its original owner? It may be euthanized or even sent to a "game ranch" to be hunted.

At Tiger Haven, the big cats roam, play, and live out their days in one of the few places in the nation designed solely for their safety and sanctuary.

The Dog Story

In 1927 a blind man in Nashville named Morris Frank heard about a program in Switzerland that trained dogs to be used by the police and the military, and as guide dogs for the Red Cross. If dogs could do that, he thought, why couldn't they be used to assist sightless people? Franks contacted Dorothy Harrison Eustis, the woman who trained the dogs in the Swiss Alps. She wasn't certain if dogs could be trained to assist blind persons, but she found a dog and trainer.

When Franks returned to Nashville with his new best friend, Buddy Fortunate Fields, called simply "Buddy," he commenced to challenge the "no dogs" rule prevalent in business establishments in the city. Stemming from this success, Franks established the Seeing Eye, the oldest guide dog school in America, now with its headquarters in New Jersey.

 # FLORA & FAUNA TRIVIA I

Q. Plans for what unique state park were announced by Governor Don Sundquist in June 1998?

A. Cumberland Trail State Park. The state's only linear park will be around 220 miles long, meandering through ten counties in Tennessee, from the Tennessee River Gorge to the Cumberland Gap National Historic Park, which is located at the Tennessee-Virginia-Kentucky border.

Q. Harcourt A. Morgan was elected to the Tennessee Agricultural Hall of Fame in 1951, in part because of his research on what two types of insects?

A. Boll weevil and cattle tick.

Q. What is the smallest of Tennessee's ducks?

A. Green-winged teal.

Q. What birds are nicknamed "fish hawks"?

A. Ospreys, which live in nests around Tennessee lakes and rivers.

Q. What natural formation in Tennessee is thirty-two miles long but undetectable from the air?

A. Cumberland Caverns, near McMinnville, the largest cave in the southeastern United States.

Q. To restore the eastern wild turkey to its previous numbers, the Tennessee Wildlife Resource Agency (TWRA) uses what procedure?

A. Hacking, which involves capturing turkeys in one area and releasing them in another.

Q. What state park is found in the center of a bustling downtown area?

A. Nashville's Bicentennial Mall, the only state park in Tennessee that's located in a city.

Q. Augustin Gattinger, who moved to Nashville from Germany as a young man, not only practiced medicine but also wrote what book on plant life in Tennessee, now regarded as a classic in its field?

A. *Tennessee Flora.*

Q. Each February, the city of Grand Junction sponsors what canine event that draws contestants from across the nation?

A. National Field Trials, held at the Ames Plantation.

Q. What is the Tennessee state fossil?

A. *Pteratrigonia (scabrotrigonia) thoracica,* which resembles a mussel. It was first dug up in Coon Creek, McNairy County.

Q. What plateau is so large that to get to Middle Tennessee early settlers traveled through Kentucky to go around it?

A. Cumberland.

Q. What is the state game bird?

A. Bobwhite quail.

Q. What is the state wildflower?

A. Passion flower.

Q. What are Tennessee's two state insects?

A. Firefly and ladybug.

Q. Thomas Sharpe Spencer, who arrived in Middle Tennessee in 1776 and was one of the earliest white settlers, spent one winter in the shelter of what kind of hollow tree?

A. A large sycamore tree, in Bledsoe County.

Q. What is the official state animal?

A. Raccoon.

Q. What is the name of the largest species of woodpecker still in existence, which nests in Tennessee?

A. Pileated woodpecker, with a height of about eighteen inches.

Since This Chapter Includes Flora . . .

Tennessee is home to an incredible abundance of plant life, a lot of it noteworthy. The variety and abundance of trees alone is enough to give Tennesseans bragging rights. In the Great Smoky Mountains National Park, there are more species of trees than in all of Europe. In the spring, lots of folks come to Tennessee just to see the wildflowers. In the fields and forests, of Tennessee you'll find virtually every wildflower there is, from arbutus and bloodroot, to trillium and yarrow (no, I couldn't find one that started with *z*).

The Chattanooga Department of Tourism says that in their area, more than three hundred kinds of trees and nine hundred varieties of wildflowers grow—and this is more than any other place on earth with the exception of Central China.

Like its neighboring states, Tennessee is partly covered with a vine that most consider a nuisance: kudzu. It drapes across old barns, nearly covering the words "See Rock City" painted on roofs, and adorns interstate signs. Brought to the South from Asia as part of an anti-erosion campaign, it has become like the four-day guest: no longer welcome. It grows at the prodigious rate of nearly a foot a day in good conditions, so you can't just cut it back and think you're done for the season. A hard frost stops it, but it never really goes away. It's so prevalent that not only have Tennesseans just about given up fighting it, they've embraced it as part of their culture. There's even a cartoon strip named *Kudzu.*

The interest in alternative medicine has brought with it research into what herbs and wildflowers (and even kudzu) can do for people. Guess what? Kudzu has been found by some medical researchers to be an effective aid in the fight against alcoholism. Maybe it'll become another of Tennessee's cash crops.

In the old days, when a Tennessean needed medicine, he or she just went out into the back yard or the nearby woods to locate the plant that would do the trick. Now it seems all of America has discovered this, but it's not "alternative medicine" to a lot of old-timers; it's just the way they've always done it.

And While We're on the Subject of Alternative Medicine . . .

The village of Red Boiling Springs is aptly named, because of the red-tinted water that was discovered there in 1830, bubbling up from the ground. Early settlers claimed this water had healing properties, and Red Boiling Springs boomed as a mineral springs resort until the Great Depression of the 1930s. Three hotels from that time have survived, and tourists still come to "take the waters." Every May, Red Boiling Springs hosts a three-day-long Folk Medicine Festival. People who visit Red Boiling Springs swear it's a cure-all—and at the very least, it's fun.

Did You Know? Sweetwater boasts the Lost Sea, the largest underground lake in the country. Here, under the guidance of the tour staff, you can ride a glass-bottomed boat and see some of the largest rainbow trout on this continent, breathtaking cave formations, and rare cave flowers called "anthodites," found in only a few caves throughout the world.

Great Smoky Mountains National Park is the largest black bear reserve in the East.
(COURTESY GREAT SMOKY MOUNTAINS NATIONAL PARK)

Unique Features of Great Smoky Mountains National Park

Nancy Gray, park spokesperson, related these intriguing facts:

★ The diversity of plants, animals, and trees is unique because of the elevation and orientation of the park (the way the mountains are positioned, going from north to south).

★ At least sixteen native mammals live there, including the black bear (the park is the largest black bear reserve in the East).

★ There are about two hundred species of birds, including the scissor-tailed flycatcher, the western kingbird, the cliff swallow, tanagers, and finches.

★ The park provides the only habitat in the world for Cain's reed-bent grass, Rugel's ragwort, and Jordan's red-cheeked salamander.

★ Within the park are over seven hundred miles of streams offering scenic beauty and housing a diversity of aquatic life.

★ Almost 95 percent of the 516,000 acres in the park is forested, with about 25 percent of the park forest never having been disturbed.

★ The park preserves a unique collection of log buildings, such as those found in Cades Cove, and it maintains seventy-five historic structures depicting various aspects of pioneer life.

A "Gem" of a Tale, or the Story of "Many Pearls"

Tipper Gore and first lady Hillary Clinton wore Tennessee pearls at President Bill Clinton's inauguration. Elizabeth Taylor visited Tennessee and

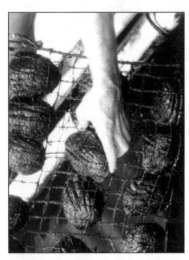

Each of these "washboard" mussels at the Birdsong pearl farm in Camden will eventually form a fresh-water pearl. (COURTESY TENNESSEE TOURIST DEVELOPMENT)

bought an exquisite strand. Others, unaware that the Tennessee state gem is the freshwater pearl, have virtually stumbled upon where the pearls are cultured. They come from the Birdsong pearl farm in tiny Camden, the only commercial pearl farm in the nation. Since the pearl farm's first days in the early 1960s, Tennessee's pearl industry has grown to a multimillion-dollar-a-year business.

It all started when South Dakota–born John Latendresse and his wife, Chessy, became interested in starting a commercial pearl farm. He had picked up a knowledge of the "musseling business" when he served in the marines in World War II and then began pearl trading along the Mississippi and Tennessee Rivers. After he and his wife studied the pearl-buying business in New York City, they decided to locate their pearl-making operation on the banks of the Tennessee River.

They chose Tennessee as the site for their pearl farm because of its moderate water temperature—fifty to seventy degrees—and for its lime content, two conditions that help set the stage for pearl production. The Latendresses spent thirty years adapting culturing techniques used on Japan's saltwater *akoya* oysters to Tennessee's freshwater mussels, and their efforts have paid off. Their operation has been written about in *National Geographic, Southern Living,* and other highly regarded national and international publications.

Neither they nor their operation's tour manager, Bob Keast, would tell exactly how they do it. Ask them and they—what else?—clam up.

No Problems with Mosquitoes Here

Every evening in the balmy months, you can go by Nickajack Cave Refuge outside Chattanooga and at dusk watch as tens of thousands of bats fly out for their supper of mosquitoes and other pests.

Strange . . . but True

A Duck's Tale

A ritual involving ducks has been happening twice a day at the Peabody Hotel in Memphis for more than sixty years now. It is here that ducks parade, marching to the large marble fountain in the lobby, waddling their way from the elevator over red carpet for a swim. This "ducky" tradition was started in 1932, when hotel manager Frank Schutt returned from a hunting trip and thought the addition of his live decoys to the lobby fountain would be an interesting touch. Making their feathery march at 11:00 A.M. and 5:00 P.M., the ducks take twice-a-day constitutionals, which have made them and the Peabody Hotel world famous.

The Tennessee Aquarium,
Where You Can See the Water Creatures of the World

The Tennessee Aquarium in Chattanooga is the largest freshwater aquarium in the world, but there's much more to it than that. There are also

huge saltwater tanks full of various kinds of sharks, stingrays, and other ocean-going creatures. All in all, a total of over nine thousand aquatic animals from around the world are under one enormous roof. Some tanks, for example, have exhibits of creatures from such varied places as the Amazon River in South America, the Volga River in Russia, and the Congo River in Africa. You can also view such animals as the Goliath bird-eating tarantula, the emperor scorpion, and the rhinoceros pit viper.

At the Tennessee Aquarium you can find such diverse aquatic creatures as river otters from the Louisiana bayou and red Oscars from the Amazon River.
(COURTESY TENNESSEE AQUARIUM; PHOTOS © 1992, 1995, 1997 BY RICHARD T. BRYANT)

When you go, make sure you are there during feeding time, when divers go into the tanks to hand-feed sharks, rays, and moray eels.

This May Be the Strangest Kitchen in the World!

Here's just a sampling of the kind of monthly grocery list needed for the kitchen at the Tennessee Aquarium to prepare food for its denizens:

★ 35,000 crickets

★ 33,300 worms

★ 1,200 pounds of restaurant-quality seafood

★ 150 rats

★ 300 mice

Mud Island River Park in Memphis features a full-scale replica of the Mississippi River.
(Courtesy Memphis Convention & Visitors Bureau)

An Island . . . Built by a Gunboat!

In 1910 a Spanish-American War gunboat headed up the Mississippi River and weighed anchor offshore at Memphis, waiting for high water to make the river more navigable. Sand, gravel, and other debris began to deposit against the hull, and months later, after the gunboat raised anchor and left, what came to be known as Mud Island continued to grow.

Over a half century later, the people of Memphis decided to make good use of the fifty-two-acre real estate in the river by constructing a park. Among other things, it now contains a five-block-long scale model of the lower Mississippi; the *Memphis Belle,* the famous World War II bomber; the River Museum containing an 1870 steamboat and part of a Union gunboat; a concert amphitheater; and swimming facilities.

Memphians certainly know how to make good use of real estate—especially when it's new real estate.

FLORA & FAUNA TRIVIA II

Q. Crossing the state twice, what river creates the three Grand Divisions of Tennessee?

A. Tennessee.

Q. What are Tennessee's two state rocks?

A. Agate and limestone.

Q. How many miles of streams does Tennessee have within its boundaries?

A. 19,000.

Q. What U.S. senator was responsible for the legislation making the Big South Fork Area a National Recreation Area?

A. Howard H. Baker Jr.

Q. Natchez Trace State Park contains the largest tree of what species, reputed to be a world record?

A. Pecan.

Q. A blue catfish caught in the Cumberland River in June 1998 weighed in at what world record?

A. 112 pounds.

Q. What is the smallest mammal in Tennessee?

A. Short-tailed shrew.

Q. What is the largest owl found in the state?

A. Great horned owl.

Q. Both Native Americans and early Tennessee settlers used an extract from the bark of what flowering tree as a cure for fevers?

A. Dogwood.

Q. In 1820 what famous naturalist and artist visited the western Tennessee area and recorded the varieties and numbers of birds he found there?

A. John James Audubon.

Q. Roan Mountain State Park contains the world's largest stand of what kind of shrub, the stands of which early settlers called "hells"?

A. Rhododendron.

Q. The Memphis Zoo was home to what famous lion until he died in 1944?

A. The Metro-Goldwyn-Mayer "roaring lion."

Q. What site has the highest underground waterfall and is the deepest cave open to tourists in the United States?

A. Ruby Falls.

Q. After whom is Ruby Falls named?

A. Ruby Lambert, wife of explorer Leo Lambert, who first discovered the falls.

Q. In what year did Congress establish the Great Smoky Mountains National Park?

A. 1934.

Q. What continuous footpath that travels from Maine to Georgia for a total length of 2,140 miles also goes through part of Tennessee?

A. The Appalachian Trail.

Q. Herman Baggenstoss began the bulletin "Turkey Feathers, Boar Bristles and Fish Fins" that evolved into the periodical *Tennessee Wildlife* and now is called by what name?

A. *The Tennessee Conservationist.*

Q. What natural stone formation is one of the largest in the world?

A. Twin Arches, in Big South Fork National River and Recreation Area. The South Arch has a clearance of 70 feet and a span of more than 135 feet; the North Arch is somewhat smaller.

1 2

Speech, Food, and Fascinating Cultrual Tidbits

The Way Tennesseans Say It

Speech patterns and grammar usage vary within the three so-called Grand Divisions of West, Middle, and East Tennessee. West Tennesseans speak with a more Deep South drawl than people in the rest of the state, while in Middle Tennessee, language patterns reveal the influence of the Kentucky Bluegrass Region. East Tennesseans' speech may be the most colorful of all, because their linguistic patterns stem from old Briticisms, which have been retained due to the relative isolation of those Tennesseans in the mountainous area of the state.

If there's one thing that sets strangers apart from locals, it's the pronunciation of *Appalachia*. Visitors usually say "Apple-AY-cha," but the "right" way is "Appah-LATCH-a."

When you come to visit people in Tennessee, it doesn't matter what your business is. You first ask them how they are, how the family is, and maybe even how their dog is (if they don't have a pet, they're sure to be renovating their car or house, or following a particular sport). After all this is out of the way, you'll probably be asked if you'd like something to drink. It might be coffee, it might be sweet iced tea, and after the sun's setting behind the nearest sycamore tree, you might be offered something stronger. Then, and only then, is it polite to discuss the reason for your visit.

This pattern of manners is one reason northerners say things move so slowly down here—but then, Tennesseans have a lot more fun taking their time.

Glossary to Help You Communicate with the Natives

A-fixing: getting ready to do something.

Aim: intend or plan. "I aim to chop wood tomorrow."

Book read: well educated; **read up on,** to study something.

Crick: something you have in your neck or back, a kind of stiffness or pain; also the pronunciation of *creek,* a small stream.

Doin's: function or event; **big doin's,** a really important function or event.

Far piece: pronounced "fur piece;" a long distance.

Fetch: bring, as in, "Fetch me that kettle."

Frog-strangler or Gully-washer: a torrential rain.

Lollygagging: loafing or loitering. "Stop your lollygagging, we've got to get to church!"

Mess of: a lot of, as in, "That's a mess of fish you got there."

Parts: usually refers to a geographical area, as in, "He's not from these parts."

Plumb: totally or completely, as in, "You look plumb tuckered out."

Poke: a container, usually a bag. "I need a poke to carry these turnip greens home in."

Put out: angry or upset, as in, "You look awful put out. What's wrong?"

Shed of: get rid of or do away with. "I'm getting shed of that coonhound tomorrow. He's no good."

Skittish: nervous or jittery. "My dog gets a little skittish in a thunder-storm."

Smack-dab: right in the middle of. (Hey, even James Taylor used this term in his song "Up on a Roof": "right smack-dab in the middle of town.")

Take a gander: look at, check out.

Tuckered out: tired.

Uppity or Biggety: someone who's being snobbish or stuck-up.

MISCELLANEOUS TRIVIA I

Q. What eight states border Tennessee?

A. Mississippi, Alabama, Georgia, North Carolina, Virginia, Kentucky, Missouri, Arkansas.

Q. What neighboring state has nine states bordering it?

A. Missouri.

Q. What is one reason that historians hypothesize that the first settlers in Tennessee were "surprisingly literate"?

A. Some of the earliest documents requiring signatures, such as the Washington District petition of 1776, show a nearly complete absence of "marks." There were signatures instead.

Q. What college preparatory school was sited on the battleground of the battle of Franklin?

A. Battle Ground Academy.

Q. Who founded Vanderbilt University?

A. Methodist bishop Holland Nimmons McTyeire and Cornelius Vanderbilt.

Q. More African Americans have earned doctorates at what Nashville university than at any other institution of higher learning in the nation?

A. Fisk.

Q. In what establishments in Nashville did the first black protesters stage lunch-counter "sit-ins" in February 1960?

A. Woolworth, Kress, and McClellan department stores.

Q. What former slave published the *Chattanooga Blade*, which in 1905 challenged Jim Crow laws and addressed other social injustices based on race?

A. Randolph Miller.

Q. At the turn of the twentieth century, a Montgomery County native pioneered the lovelorn, or advice, column in the *New Orleans Picayune* using what pseudonym?

A. Dorothy Dix.

Q. Murfreesboro author Mary Noailles Murfree wrote many novels using

Tennessee mountain settings, including *The Frontiersman, In the Tennessee Mountains*, and *In the Clouds*, using what male pen name?

A. Charles E. Craddock.

Q. In 1986 what writer, raised in Clarksville, became the first poet laureate of the United States?

A. Robert Penn Warren.

Q. An enormous bronze statue of what author stands in Morningside Park, Knoxville?

A. Alex Haley, author of *Roots,* who made Knoxville his home.

Q. In 1935 how did author David Cohn define the Mississippi Delta?

A. "The Mississippi Delta begins in the lobby of the Peabody Hotel and ends on Catfish Row in Vicksburg."

Q. In 1905, what popular short story writer visited Nashville and wrote the following description of the city in his "Municipal Report"? "Take London fog 30 parts; malaria 10 parts; gas leaks 20 parts; dewdrops gathered in a brick yard at sunrise, 25 parts; odor of honeysuckle 15 parts. Mix."

A. O. Henry.

Q. What modern-day Cherokee author's words are emblazoned in the marble River Wall of the Bicentennial Capitol Mall in Nashville?

A. Marilou Awiakta, born in Knoxville in 1936, whose book *Selu: Seeking the Corn-Mother's Wisdom* applied Native American philosophy to modern-day issues.

Q. Poet Leonard Tate's poem "Mountain People" immortalized what small village in Tennessee?

A. Beersheba Springs.

Home Cookin'

No matter where you go in Tennessee, food is important. Some health-conscious, well-meaning soul might try to explain how bad some of the traditional foods are, from a health standpoint. That person might get enlightened to the fact that most Tennesseans were raised on fried catfish and hushpuppies, fried okra and cornbread with chitlins, and Lumberjack Special breakfasts. Plus, an old relative (Great-Aunt Eloise or Great-Uncle Augustus) ate this every day of her or his life and lived to a ripe old age, never spent a day in the hospital, and died smoking a pipe to boot. Tennesseans like their barbecue, country ham, biscuits and cornbread, sweet tea, and turnip greens and black-eyed peas with bacon drippings. You'll see food like this at all kinds of events: cemetery-decorating days, family reunions, tailgate parties, and church potlucks.

On the TV show *Hee Haw,* the late great Grandpa Jones would answer the question, "What's for supper?" These are the foods that most Tennesseans probably had on the table as he reeled off his menu.

The Vilest-Smelling, Sweetest-Tasting Weed in East Tennessee

Every April the people in Polk County have their Annual Ramp Festival. The ramp is a wild onion-like plant of the *Allium* family that grows only in the Appalachian Mountains.

For Tennesseans, that's special enough to celebrate, with craft shows, lots of live bluegrass and country music, and, of course, plenty of ramps to eat (and they're in just about everything except maybe the ice cream). President Truman was the guest of honor at the very first Ramp Festival in 1954.

Here's how you cook 'em:

Holland Reese's Ramps and Eggs

Rinse ramps with cool water until they are really clean; then chop them. Heat bacon grease until very hot in large iron skillet. Place chopped ramps in skillet and cook for 25 to 30 minutes. Add three dozen scrambled eggs, salt to taste, and heat. Serve with bacon and fried cornbread.

When Tennessee Was Host to the World

In June 1976, Nashville hosted a meeting of the entire United Nations, including ambassadors, their bodyguards, and their families. This was the only time the United Nations has ever met socially in the United States outside of New York. The meeting was all top secret until a few weeks before, with media coverage coordinated by Brooks Parker, press secretary for Governor Ray Blanton.

Food preparation, to serve more than sixteen hundred, was overseen by chef Phila Hach of Montgomery County. She served them traditional southern fare. The United Nations enjoyed mint julep frappé, Tennessee country ham, catfish and hush puppies, southern fried chicken, cornbread, green beans with ham hocks, corn on the cob, and Hach's famous southern pecan pie (see recipe below). The meal was served in Centennial Park.

Recipes You Might Want to Try

Every good cook in the Volunteer State will tell you his or her recipe for their favorite dish is the best. Here are just a few:

Phila Hach's Best Pecan Pie in the World

3 eggs

1 teaspoon vanilla

3 tablespoons melted margarine

½ teaspoon salt

½ cup sugar

1 cup Karo syrup

1 cup chopped pecans

1 unbaked pie crust

Beat eggs slightly. Add vanilla, margarine, salt, sugar, and Karo syrup. Blend well. Add chopped pecans. Pour in pie crust. Bake for 12 minutes at 375°; reduce heat to 325° and continue baking until pie is set.

Vernon Summerlin's Gar Balls and Rusty Gravy

Vernon Summerlin, the editor of *Tennessee Angler Magazine,* is the author of many books, including a cookbook on preparing game. This recipe works equally well with alligator gar or catfish.

2½ pounds gar (or catfish), ground

½ cup bell peppers, ground

2 cups water

2 eggs

1 pound whole tomatoes

1 cup onions, ground

2 tablespoons salt

1 teaspoon black pepper

½ cup oil, plus extra for browning

1½ cups flour, plus extra for dusting

Thoroughly mix all the ingredients in a large bowl. Shape into large balls, dust with flour, and brown, using oil, in a heavy skillet. Cook until done.

Gravy

3 tablespoons flour

tomato juice (enough to make desired consistency)

2 cups water

In a skillet brown flour, tomato juice, and water. Crumble two fish balls into gravy, stirring well to make heavy gravy. Add remaining fish balls to gravy, being careful not to break them. Cover skillet and simmer 30 minutes. Serve gravy over hot rice. Serves around 6.

Venison Sauerbraten with Gingersnap Gravy

This is my own recipe, which appeared in Vernon Summerlin's book on game cooking.

3-to-4-pound venison roast

2 red onions, diced

3 bay leaves

12 peppercorns

6 whole cloves

3 teaspoons salt

1¾ cups red wine vinegar (or apple cider vinegar)

1 cup boiling water

2 tablespoons bacon drippings or shortening

12 gingersnap cookies, crushed to make at least ¾ cup

2 teaspoons brown sugar

Put roast in a glass bowl or crock with onions, bay leaves, peppercorns, cloves, salt, vinegar, and boiling water. Cover with a tight-fitting lid; refrigerate for at least three days. Turn the roast twice a day in the marinade.

After three days, remove meat, saving marinade. Sear roast in heavy skillet on all sides. Put in a slow electric cooker or large, heavy pot, and pour the marinade over the meat.

Cover tightly, bring to a boil, and simmer for around 3½ hours or until meat is tender. Remove roast from the pot and keep it warm while you make the gravy.

To make gingersnap gravy, strain the simmered marinade. Add water, if needed, to make 2½ cups liquid. Cover and simmer 10 minutes; then add crushed gingersnaps and brown sugar. Simmer for another 5 minutes.

Pass gravy with roast and pour over potatoes or rice, and meat.

Tennessee Barbecue Sauce, Jack Daniel's Style

1 medium onion, finely chopped

1 clove garlic, minced

2 tablespoons vegetable oil

1½ cups catsup

¼ cup brown sugar

2 tablespoons Jack Daniel's whiskey

1 teaspoon liquid smoke

2½ tablespoons cider vinegar

½ teaspoon dry mustard

2 drops hot pepper sauce

Sauté onion and garlic in vegetable oil until tender. Stir in the remaining ingredients and bring to a boil over medium heat. Reduce heat and simmer for 10 minutes. Makes about 2 cups. Great for chicken, pork, and beef.

A Little about Poke Salad

This coarse perennial herb's botanical name is *Phytolacca americana,* but old-timers in Tennessee call the edible green "poke sallet." It grows wild in the woods and fields and although the root is said to be poisonous, the tender green leaves and young stems are delicious when cooked tender. Some people strip the stalk on the older plants; cut it in half-inch pieces; roll it in meal, salt, and pepper; and fry it as they would okra. Whether it's called poke salad or poke sallet, it's worth a try.

Old-timer's Poke Salad

This recipe was told to me by an old Appalachian woman who said, "Honey, please don't bother folks about my name. Just give 'em the recipe." So I'm telling you just what she said:

"The trick of it is to pick the poke while it's tender . . . about a foot high, I'd say, in late April when it's the best. You pick your poke, stems and leaves, while it's young, about 2 pounds of that. After you wash it, you put it in about 2 or 3 quarts of water. Make sure it's covered with the water, and boil it till it's tender. Then take a big colander and pour the poke and water in it and drain it. Squeeze out all the moisture, as much as you can. Have you an iron skillet, that's the best, about a 10- or 12-inch skillet. Get your bacon drippings, about a half a cup of bacon drippings, and put it in there. Add your drained poke salad; break it apart with your hands as you add it. Cook it good in the grease, about 5 or 10 minutes in there.

"Break 6 eggs in a bowl, mix them with a fork, and pour that with your salt and pepper into the poke in the skillet. Cook the eggs and mix it with the poke until they're done. It's really good. You can also take the bacon and crumble it over. Some people put a little minced onion, but old-timers don't do it that way.

"We'll have this for supper with hot cornbread and fresh churned butter and sweet tea. There's nothin' better."

Prize-Winning Cornbread

At South Pittsburg's annual National Cornbread Festival the last weekend in April, the Cornbread Cook-off usually gets around seven hundred entries. Usually one hundred thousand people attend the festivities, which include music, crafts, children's activities, and, of course, cornbread. Festival executive board member Beth Duggar gave me this winning recipe.

Reuben Casserole with Cornbread

1 (27-ounce) can sauerkraut, drained

2 medium tomatoes, thinly sliced

⅓ cup Thousand Island salad dressing

⅓ cup sliced black olives, drained

2 tablespoons butter or margarine

9 ounces sliced corned beef, shredded

2 cups shredded Swiss cheese

1 cup Martha White cornmeal mix

⅓ cup Martha White self-rising flour

1 teaspoon sugar

1 egg, slightly beaten

1 cup buttermilk

⅓ cup whole milk (or 2 percent)

3 tablespoons oil

Heat oven to 425°. Spread sauerkraut in ungreased cast-iron skillet. Arrange tomato slices over sauerkraut; spread with salad dressing; dot with 2 tablespoons butter and sprinkle with black olives. Top with corned beef and cheese. Bake for 15 minutes.

While casserole is baking, combine cornmeal, flour, sugar, egg, buttermilk, milk, and oil. Stir until well mixed. Remove skillet from oven. Pour cornbread mixture over baked mixture. Return to oven and bake for 15 to 20 minutes or until cornbread is golden brown.

Serve with Quick Mustard Sauce, if desired. Serves 6 to 8.

Quick Mustard Sauce

½ cup mayonnaise

½ teaspoon prepared mustard

1 teaspoon finely chopped onion

Combine all ingredients. Makes 1 cup.

Bill's Catfish House Recipes

If you drive to Ashland City, you'll find Bill's Catfish House, which serves the best catfish in Tennessee. Bill Krantz gave me a couple of recipes, one for catfish and one for hushpuppies. "I turned Dinah Shore down when she asked me for some recipes for one of her cookbooks," he told me at first. Somehow I got these out of him.

Hushpuppies

1 cup meal

½ cup flour

¼ cup ground onion

¼ cup sharp cheddar cheese, grated

1 "pony" size Budweiser

1 egg

buttermilk

Mix that all together until it's real thick, like you would for making a cake. Let it stand for about 15 minutes. Drop the hushpuppy dough by spoonfuls into hot grease, cook 'em until they're done. Drain and serve them with catfish.

Catfish

2 cups cracker meal

1 cup self-rising flour

2 tablespoons Cajun seasoning (like Tony Cachere's)

½ teaspoon garlic

Mix all this well and batter your catfish fillets in it. Fry 'em up in deep fat for 3 to 5 minutes, depending on thickness of the fillets. Serve with hushpuppies.

Are You Hungry Tonight? Order Barbecue.

No matter where you travel in Tennessee, even the most remote hamlet will have a barbecue stand. It's also interesting the way barbecue dishes vary depending on where in the state you travel. In East Tennessee there is "pulled" pork, which is pulled off the bone before serving. In Middle

Tennessee you'll find primarily pulled pork and ribs. But it's in West Tennessee that the controversy of wet versus dry ribs is a big deal. *Dry* means the meat hasn't been basted with a sauce and is treated with dry seasonings. *Wet* is basted with barbecue sauces of all kinds. You'll find aficionados of pulled, wet, and dry barbecue just about everywhere.

And for true barbecue lovers, forget about barbecued chicken or beef. As one barbecue chef quipped, "If it ain't pork, it ain't barbecue."

Braggin' Rights

Here are some of Tennessee's claims to fame:

★ **World's largest pencil:** in Shelbyville, made by the city's pencil manufacturer, Sanford Corporation.

★ **One of the last true grasslands:** Coffee County's May Prairie.

★ **Most visited home in the nation, after the White House:** Graceland, Elvis's palatial mansion in Memphis, which in 1991 was listed with the National Register of Historic Places.

★ **First full admiral in the U.S. Navy:** Knoxville native and Civil War hero David Glasgow Farragut, who was promoted to vice admiral in 1866 by act of Congress.

★ **World's longest paper clip chain:** measures 18.22 miles and was made by Clarksville High School students on April 18, 1999, as a fund-raiser to buy computers for an orphanage in Mexico.

★ **World's first self-service grocery store:** introduced by Clarence Saunders, who opened his first Piggly Wiggly store in Memphis in 1916.

Graceland, Elvis's Memphis mansion, receives more visitors than any other home in the nation, other than the White House. (COURTESY MEMPHIS CONVENTION & VISITORS BUREAU)

★ **Nation's oldest continuously run weight-for-age steeplechase:** the Iroquois Steeplechase in Nashville's Percy Warner Park every May, which started back in 1941.

★ **First American surgeon to perform a hysterectomy:** Dr. Paul Fitzsimmons Eve, professor of surgery at the University of Nashville from 1851 to 1861 and from 1870 to 1877.

★ **World's steepest railroad:** Chattanooga's Incline Railway, which takes visitors to see Rock City at the top of Lookout Mountain.

★ **Oldest registered distillery in America:** Jack Daniel's in Lynchburg.

★ **Member of the first sheep-cloning team:** Erin native Dr. J. Lannett Edwards, a reproductive biologist and embryologist who for a time worked with the Scottish cloning team that produced Dolly, the cloned sheep. "If only I could clone the experience!" said the enthusiastic Dr. Edwards.

★ **The undisputed title "pork barbecue capital of the world":** claimed by Memphis.

★ **Highest sheer-drop waterfall east of the Mississippi River:** Fall Creek Falls near Cookeville (at 256 feet, for those who really need a number).

★ **Only bridge of its kind in the United States (and one of only two in the world):** the post-tensioned, segmental concrete double-arch bridge on the Natchez Trace Parkway over Highway 96, southwest of Nashville. It looks like a work of art (and an expensive one, too, at a cost of $12 million).

★ **Postmaster general who introduced the postage stamp to the nation:** Tennessean Cave Johnson, postmaster general during the administration of James K. Polk, another Tennessean.

★ **Greatest collection of Victorian literature in America:** at the Thomas Hughes Library in Rugby.

★ **World's second-largest Eiffel Tower:** in Paris, Tennessee. Built to scale at Christian Brothers University in Memphis, for Memphis in May's 1990 salute to France, the tower is sixty-five feet tall and is made of five hundred pieces of Douglas fir and six thousand steel rods.

The Eiffel Tower in Paris, Tennessee, is the second largest Eiffel Tower in the world. (COURTESY DR. J. CURT TAYLOR, O.D., PARIS, TENN.)

★ **The title "pumpkin capital of the world":** claimed by Pikeville in Bledsoe County.

★ **Worst earthquake in U.S. history:** formed Reelfoot Lake in West Tennessee in 1812.

★ **World's largest freshwater aquarium:** the Tennessee Aquarium in Chattanooga. It is the height of a twelve-story building, measures 130,000 square feet in size, and holds approximately 400,00 gallons of water.

★ **World's largest country music research center:** the Country Music Foundation in Nashville.

★ **Best place to live for starting a rock band:** Memphis, according to *Swing* magazine's 1997 nationwide survey, because "starving musicians can benefit from the low cost of living while enjoying plenty of cheap barbecued pork."

★ **Largest knife store in the world:** Smoky Mountain Knife Works in Sevierville, which houses a knife museum and also claims to have Tennessee's largest collection of mounted heads on its walls.

★ **World's biggest fish fry:** held every April in Paris, when they cook more than 12,500 pounds of catfish—that's well over six tons!

★ **World's largest outdoor barbecue:** the annual Irish Picnic and Homecoming, held the last weekend in July in the tiny town of McEwen (population approximately 1,450). Begun in 1854, the barbecue is hosted by St. Patrick Church and School and is attended by over 20,000 people, who eat more than 20,000 pounds of pork and 2,100 whole chickens, plus fixin's.

★ **The title "nursery capital of the world":** claimed by Warren County, which has more than four hundred nursery growers within its boundaries.

★ **World's only exact-size replica of the ancient temple the Parthenon in Athens, Greece:** Nashville's Parthenon, situated in Centennial Park. In keeping with Nashville's reputation as "the Athens of the South," it was originally built to celebrate Tennessee's Centennial Exposition. Inside you'll find a fourty-two-foot-tall statue of the Greek goddess Athena.

★ **Possibly the world's oldest cooking grease still in use:** in Dyer's Cafe in Bartlett. The present owner, Jim Marshall, says Elmer Dyer started with the original grease in 1912 when he was cooking and serving from a covered wagon. Marshall strains the grease twice a day, and it is so special he uses a police escort whenever the twelve-gallon grease vat is moved.

MISCELLANEOUS TRIVIA II

Q. Why did Nashvillians call June 20, 1873, "Black Friday"?

A. On that day, seventy-two deaths resulted from the cholera epidemic in the city.

Q. What Nashville-born astronomer, a pioneer in celestial photography, published over 4,000 astronomical photographs, wrote more than 840 articles related to the study of space, and discovered 16 comets and Jupiter's fifth moon?

A. Edward Emerson Barnard, whose first photographs were published in 1913.

Q. Born in Humphreys County, U.S. Navy Captain William Robert Anderson was the first to accomplish what feat in 1958?

A. Commanded the nuclear-powered *Nautilus,* the first submarine to sail under the ice at the North Pole.

Q. Where did scientist Persa Raymond Bell pioneer a scanner that, when used with ingested radioactive substances, helped diagnose cancers and other diseases without surgical intervention?

A. Oak Ridge National Laboratory.

Q. What advocate of the use of quinine in the treatment of malaria wrote the first medical book to be published west of the Mississippi River?

A. Nashville physician Dr. John Sappington, who published his *Theory and Treatment of Fevers* in 1844 in Missouri.

Q. Greene County physician John Harvey Girdner is best known for being the first to successfully perform what surgical procedure?

A. Grafting a dead person's skin onto a living person.

Q. In 1816 what noted artist from the Northeast came to the Hermitage to paint Andrew Jackson's portrait, married Rachel Jackson's niece, and lived the rest of his life in Nashville?

A. Ralph E. W. Earl.

Q. What transplanted Scotsman, settling in Chattanooga, made a name for himself as a painter of panoramic landscapes?

A. John Cameron, whose *Colonel Whiteside and Family* now hangs in the Hunter Museum of Art in Chattanooga.

Q. Who was the state's first notable African American artist?

A. Aaron Douglass of Fisk University, where some of his important works are exhibited.

Q. What Tennessee artist was forced to leave the state because of his wife's strong abolitionist stance?

A. John Wood Dodge.

Q. In 1872 who painted *Smoky Mountain Wedding*, which, because of its stereotypical characterizations of African Americans and mountain folks, is said to have been painted in deference to northerners' expectations?

A. John Stokes, whose painting now hangs in the Tennessee State Museum.

Q. Who is considered Tennessee's most notable impressionistic artist?

A. Catherine Wiley of Knoxville. Her work is exhibited both in the state and in the Metropolitan Museum of Art in New York.

Q. What did early Native Americans use to seal their baskets so they could hold water?

A. Tree gum.

Q. What is the most popular form of basket being made today as a Tennessee craft?

A. Ribbed baskets, made with strips of white oak.

Q. What is the nation's most visited national park?

A. Great Smoky Mountains National Park.

Q. What is the nation's largest national historical park?

A. Cumberland Gap National Historical Park, situated at the convergence of Kentucky, Tennessee, and Virginia.

13

Unusual Grave and Burial-Site Stories

The Enduring Lure of Nannie Taylor's Shrine

In Clarksville, just northwest of Nashville, there once lived a little girl named Nannie Taylor, the daughter of Judge Charles W. and Molly Taylor, who were wealthy and respected in the community. Born in 1881, "Little Nannie" died of pneumonia when she was only four years old.

In those days, if you had anything special done in the way of burial sculptures, it was done in France, so the grieving father sent a photo of Nannie and ordered an exact replica of her.

The statue was intricately carved in marble, even down to her little teeth, delicate dimpled hands, and the lace on her pantaloons. Frozen in time, Nannie stood in Greenwood Cemetery until 1996, when her statue was stolen. The Taylor family appealed for its return, and the story of the search for Nannie's statue made national television.

In Boston, an antiques dealer was watching the news and thought the statue looked familiar. Sure enough, he had it for sale in his shop. The dealer drove it back to Clarksville, where there was a rededication ceremony, complete with a speech from the mayor.

For a while Nannie's statue became a kind of shrine. It was decorated with necklaces, toys, knickknacks, and, depending on the season, a Christmas tree

For a while, the statue of Nannie Taylor became a sort of shrine, with visitors leaving tokens at "her" feet. (PHOTO BY THE AUTHOR)

or Easter lily. Some visitors apparently hoped Nannie could help them with an illness of a loved one, for they often left family photographs at "her" feet!

After it received so much attention, the statue was knocked over (either accidentally or deliberately) and one arm was broken off. Now it is protected in a building near the cemetery.

✪ Strange . . . but True

These Confederate Soldiers Moved to Missouri—after They Died!

In Lake County, near Reelfoot Lake, approximately seventy-five Confederate soldiers were buried in a cemetery near where they fell at the 1862 battle of Island No. 10. Several years after they were buried, the Mississippi River changed course, and the island on which the soldiers are buried is now part of Missouri.

The Mysterious Death of Meriwether Lewis

The burial site of Meriwether Lewis, the coleader of the Lewis and Clark Expedition, lies near the tiny village of Hohenwald, in Lewis County, which is named for him. At first he was honored for his brave exploration across the American continent, but his problems began after he was named governor of the Louisiana Territory and questions were raised in Congress about his account-keeping. Dismayed and deeply depressed by these charges, Lewis was on his way from St. Louis to Washington along the Natchez Trace to defend himself. At sunset on October 11, 1810, he reached Grinder's Stand, an inn owned by Robert Grinder, who was away from home. Mrs. Grinder provided lodging for Lewis and his two servants.

How he died that night is still a mystery. Some say he was murdered for the boxes he carried, which contained documents, not money. Other people speculate that he shot himself. At any rate, at daylight he was found, still conscious but fatally wounded, with a piece of his forehead blown off. He died soon after.

Captain Lewis is buried where he died, and the site is a National Landmark in the Meriwether Lewis Park at mile marker 385.9 on the Natchez Trace. The grave monument is in the shape of a broken column, a symbol of a life ended before it was fully lived.

Meriwether Lewis, coleader of the Lewis and Clark Expedition, lies buried along the Natchez Trace, near Hohenwald and the inn at which he died. (COURTESY TENNESSEE STATE MUSEUM PHOTOGRAPHIC ARCHIVES)

The Largest Private Cemetery in the Nation

The small town of Franklin, and the peaceful home known as Carnton Plantation, were to become the backdrop for one of the most decisive and bloody battles of the Civil War. Carnton Plantation would also go on to become the site of the largest private cemetery in the United States because of the battle of Franklin.

Carnton Plantation was built around 1826 by Irishman Randal McGavock, a former mayor of Nashville. In 1848 his son John married Carrie Winder, and they lived on the plantation, raising wheat, corn, oats, and thoroughbred horses. They had two children, Hattie and Winder.

When the battle of Franklin burst upon their world, their home was one of forty-four in the area that became field hospitals and morgues. Many of Franklin's citizens volunteered to help with the casualties. The McGavock children, nine-year-old Hattie and seven-year-old Winder, assisted the surgeons and helped tend the wounded. One can only guess at the atrocities their young eyes saw then: the dead were stacked, according to one account, "like cordwood" on the porch and in the yard around the house, and the wood floor became stained with blood that is still visible today.

Their mother, Carrie, worked tirelessly with surgeons from the regiments to save whomever she could, but there were so many casualties it was impossible to treat them all. Four dead Confederate generals were laid out on Carnton's back porch: Cleburne, Granbury, Strahl, and Adams. The dark day of November 30, 1864, saw more than fifteen hundred Confederate soldiers die within four hours at Carnton Mansion; thousands more died in the following weeks from complications and poor hygiene.

But that was far from the end of the story. The Union dead were buried where they fell, then later claimed by friends or relatives, or reinterred in national cemeteries. Over 1,750 Confederate dead remained buried on the battlefield. Wooden headstones indicated these soldiers' names, companies, and regiments, but as time went on, the inscriptions began to fade away.

Steadfast in their role as hosts, the McGavock family set aside two acres of their land and reinterred each soldier there, buried by state of origin. In her own hand, Carrie recorded the information from each original wooden marker; her list became known as the Register of the Dead. The family gave each grave a new cedar headstone, and the Register of the Dead is now the property of the Historic Carnton Association. Because of the foresight and patriotism of Carrie McGavock, the memories of those fallen soldiers will never fade.

Did You Know? In 1862 President Abraham Lincoln signed a bill creating national cemeteries "for the soldiers who shall die in service of the country." After the Civil War, recovery teams worked to disinter the remains of about 250,000 Union soldiers from makeshift burial sites. By 1870 the remains were properly reburied by the federal government in seventy-three different national cemeteries. Individual states of the old Confederacy were responsible for preparing and maintaining cemeteries for Southern soldiers.

Guarding "Our Forefathers' Bones"

In Chattanooga some grave sites that are not tourist attractions are guarded by a special patrol deputized by the Hamilton County sheriff's office.

Ancient Native American burial places in around six hundred acres of Chattanooga's Moccasin Bend were being destroyed. In the 1970s alone, more than eight hundred burial sites were looted or vandalized.

Alarmed by the desecration, a group of Native Americans approached the sheriff to see what could be done to stop it. The sheriff told them he did not have enough personnel for such a task as guarding the forests and fields along the Tennessee River.

Thus Cherokees Robert DeBord and Gary Williams formed their own patrol, the Native American Reserve Force of Hamilton County, and became deputized. The sheriff's office has since reported grave vandalism as nearly eliminated, and according to state archaeologist Nick Fielder, there is no other such reserve force in the country.

The Tale of the Missing Grave

The French-Canadian fur trader Timothe Boucher de Montbrun became one of Nashville's first white settlers when his pirogue slipped along the Shauvanon River (now called the Cumberland River) in 1769.

The young man lived for a time in a cave above the river in the area known as French Lick and formed friendships with the Cherokee, Chickasaw, and Creek, who traded their furs for wares he could supply. He served in the military as a lieutenant governor in command of the Northwest Territory, after which he opened a mercantile business on Nashville's Public Square. He had anglicized his name to Demonbreun, the name of a Nashville street today, and had two wives: one in Illinois and one in Nashville.

When he died in 1826, his obituary in the November edition of the *Nashville Banner & Nashville Whig* read simply, "On Monday evening last, Capt. Timothy DeMumbrane, a venerable citizen of Nashville, and the first white man that ever emigrated to this vicinity." No mention was made of the place of burial.

Timothy Demonbreun's grave has never been found. Some historians say he was buried in the old North Nashville Cemetery (near what today is Fourth Avenue North). Others say his remains were reburied in City Cemetery. Still others think his remains were never moved and are now buried in the back of what used to be a blacksmith shop on Jefferson Street. Finally, his descendants erected a marker next to that of his common-law wife in a cemetery near Ashland City.

In 1996 another monument to Demonbreun was erected by the city of Nashville to commemorate its "first citizen." The 8-foot-tall, 650-pound bronze statue stands near Fort Nashborough; it was sculpted by Germantown resident Alan LeQuire, who also created the statue of Athena in the Parthenon.

A "Capitol" Burial Site

Who's buried in the capitol in Nashville? Two people, to be exact. One is William Strickland, a noted Philadelphia architect who came to Nashville in 1845 to oversee construction of the building. The process was long and laborious, and Strickland even had to resort to using prisoners from the state penitentiary to save on labor expenses.

The General Assembly was able to meet in the capitol in October 1853, although construction was not yet complete. The legislators designated a burial place for Strickland at the northeast wall of the north basement portico.

Strickland died six weeks later and is entombed in the place set aside in honor of "his genius in erecting so grand a work." Also buried in the capitol is Samuel Morgan, the only member of the Capitol Commission to serve during the entire time of the building's construction.

Did You Know? **?** Fort Donelson National Cemetery is Tennessee's most diverse cemetery. It is the burial place of veterans of seven different wars.

Intriguing Obituaries

Here are some interesting obituaries from earlier Tennessee newspapers.

★ **Jenkins.** Died recently at LaGrange Ironworks, in Stewart County. A horse thief and a bigamist—had three living wives. Asked that this be published after his death.

★ **(No name.)** 1877. Died in a runaway wagon caused by yellow jackets stinging his mules.

★ **Weaver.** 25 April 1877. Murdered by his wife at Dover Furnace, Stewart Co., Tn. Married three days prior to being murdered on Saturday.

★ (**No name.**) 1878. Died of suffocation in a cotton house.

★ **Miss Laura Bradley.** 7 June 1879. Died in Paris, Tn. Buried in her wedding dress which was to be worn in a few weeks.

★ **Davidson** [no indication whether this is a name or the county]. 10 June 1882. By wheels of a passing ice wagon on Main Street, loaded with 1,000 pounds of ice.

★ **Whitfield.** Died about 1883 in the outhouse at the rear of Southern Hotel.

★ **William J. Green.** 15 January 1883. Among first to enlist in the Civil War. First to reach home after the surrender of the war.

★ **Mrs. Eveline Reeves.** 16 Feb. 1885. Aged. Accidentally walked off the platform of a sleeper, attached to a train. On the way to Topeka, Kansas. Had ten children with her.

★ **James Thomason.** 4 June 1892. Killed at VanLeer by station agent Daniel, self-defense. Dispute over a bicycle.

★ **Mrs. Rachel Jackson Lawrence.** Died at her "Birdsong" country home near Nashville, Tn. Daughter of Andrew Jackson's adopted son. Last surviving member of The Hermitage household of "Old Hickory's" time.

★ **Lucy Nelle Dickinson.** 9 March 1917. Hit by an auto on Poston Street. First death caused by a[n] automobile, that was published in the newspaper.

★ **D. Harvey Welch.** 7 July 1928. Killed by a shotgun blast while climbing a fence to chase a skunk out of the okra patch, St. Bethlehem.

★ **Hamilton.** 14 July 1929. Died of tin-tainted milk in Houston County, Tn.

★ **Thomas Edward McReynolds.** 10 Mar. 1929. Clarksville's First Licensed Embalmer.

 # GRAVEYARD TRIVIA

Q. In what Memphis cemetery are buried fourteen Confederate generals, two governors, three U.S. senators, and twenty-one city mayors?

A. Elmwood, on South Dudley Street.

Q. Where is the mother of Sam Houston, Elizabeth Paxton Houston, buried?

A. Maryville, in the cemetery at Baker's Creek Church.

Q. What soldier credited with firing the first shot against the British in the battle of Kings Mountain is buried in the Bean-Raulston Graveyard in Marion County?

A. Captain Robert Bean.

Q. In what city cemetery do the remains of more than twenty thousand early settlers, including James Robertson and Governor William Carroll, have their final resting place?

A. City Cemetery, in Nashville, at 4th Avenue South and Oak Street.

Q. How many national cemeteries are in Tennessee?

A. Five, in Memphis, Chattanooga, Mountain Home, Knoxville, and Nashville.

VIRTUAL TENNESSEE

The following is a list of selected websites pertaining to Tennessee. Keep in mind that often you no longer need to type in the old "http://" or even "www." Most of the time, simply typing in something like "tvrail.com" will give you what you want. In addition, none of these sites are case-sensitive—type in all caps or all lowercase and you should get there. The comprehensive sites are just that: they have everything or link to many other topics relating to the Volunteer State. Many counties and even small towns have their own web pages; you can usually find links to these through the State of Tennessee web page. For sites not listed here, you can usually type a few key words into your favorite search engine and go from there.

I have checked these sites prior to publication, but can provide no guarantees against pages that cannot be displayed, changes of website addresses (if you find any, let me know), or computer glitches. I do, however, hope these addresses will give you a foot up in your virtual research.

Comprehensive Sites with Links

Everything Tennessee: www.10esc.com

General: www.volstate.net/

List of Contacts, Departments, Ad Infinitum*:
    www.state.tn.us/contact/html

State of Tennessee: www.state.tn.us/

Tennessee Association of Business: www.tennbiz.org

Tennessee Department of Economic and Community Development:
    www.state.tn.us/ecd/

---

*This site is so comprehensive that if you can't find it here, you don't really need it.

Tennessee Department of Education: www.state.tn.us/education

Tennessee Department of Transportation: www.state.tn.us/transport/

Tennessee Official City Sites: www. officialcitysites.org/tennessee.htm

Tennessee State Library and Archives:
www.state.tn.us/sos/statelib/tslahome.htm

Major City Websites

Chattanooga: www.chattanooga.net

Clarksville (and Montgomery County): www.clarksville.tn.us

Gatlinburg Tourism: www.gatlinburg-tennessee.com

Knoxville: www.knoxville.org

Memphis: www.comtutors.com/memlink.htm

Nashville: www.nashville.org/

Nature, Hunting, Hiking, Fishing, Sports

Appalachian Trail Conference: www.atconf.org

Cherokee National Forest: www.r8web.com/

English Mountain Llama Treks: www.hikinginthesmokies.com

General Sports: www.findit-sports.com

Golf: www.beartrace.com, www.anancyweb.com/tennessee.html

Hohenwald Elephant Sanctuary: www.iu5.org/imts/elephant.htm

Land between the Lakes National Recreation Area: www2.lbl.org/lbl

Legends Golf Club: www.tndirectory.com/legends

Lookout Mountain Hang Gliding: www.hanglide.com

NASCAR: www.nascar.com/

Ober Gatlinburg Skiing: www.obergatlinburg.com

Ocoee Whitewater Center: www.r8web.com/ocoee

Recreation Opportunities on Federal Lands: www.recreation.gov

Smoky Mountain Visitors Center: www.smokymountains.org

Tennessee College Sports: www.totalcollegesports.com

Tennessee Deer Hunter: www.tndeer.com

Tennessee Department of Tourist Development: www.state.tn.us/tourdev

Tennessee Scenic River Association: www.paddletsra.org

Tennessee State Parks: www.tnstateparks.com,
    www.state.tn.us/environment/parks/

Tennessee Titans (NFL team): www.tennessee-titanfans.com

Tennessee Walking Horses/The Celebration:
    www.walking-horse.com/celebration.html

Tennessee Wildlife Nature Center: www.tnwildlifecenter.org

Tennessee Wildlife Resources Agency: www.state.tn.us/twra/index.html

Trail Sites (general): www.tennesseetrails.org/

UT Sports: www.utsports.com

Women's Basketball Hall of Fame: www.wbhof.com

Film, Entertainment, Music

Beale Stree: www.bealestreet.com

Country Music Hall of Fame and Museum: www.country.com/home

Gaylord Entertainment's Country Music Page: www.musiccountry.com

Grand Ole Opry: www.opry.com

MCA: www.mca-nashville.com

Nashville Music: www.nashvillemusic.com

Sony Music: www.sonymusic.com/labels/nashville

Tennessee Film, Entertainment, and Music Commission: www.state.tn.us/film/

W. C. Handy Awards: www.handyawards.com

Western Beat Entertainment: www.westernbeat.com

WSM-AM: www.wsmonline.com

History, Art, Museums, Railroads

American Museum of Science and Energy: www.amse.org

Arrowmont School of Arts and Crafts: www.arrowmont.org

Casey Jones Home & Museum: www.caseyjones.com

Cheekwood Botanical Gardens and Museum of Art: www.cheekwood.org/

Civil War in Tennessee: www.civilwar.org

Clarksville-Montgomery County Museum: www.clarksville.tn.us

East Tennessee Historical Society Museum: www.east-tennessee-history.org

The Farm: www.thefarm.org

Fort Campbell Military Reservation/Don F. Pratt Museum*:
    www.campbell.army/mil/pratt/http://

Frank H. McClung Museum: www.mcclungmuseum.utk.edu/

Hunter Museum of American Art: www.huntermuseum.org

Knoxville Museum of Art: www.knoxart.org

Lookout Mountain Incline Railway: www.lookoutmtnattractions.com

McMinn County Living Heritage Museum: www.usit.com/livher/

National Medal of Honor Museum of Military History:
    www.smoky.com/medalofhonor/

Southern Appalachia Railway Museum:
    www.techscribes.com/sarm/sarm.htm

Tennessee Antebellum Trail: www.citysearch.com/nas/antebellumtrail

Tennessee Backroads Heritage: www.tennweb.com/tnbkrds/

Tennessee's Only On-Line Magazine: www.tennesseehistory.com

Tennessee State Museum (Tennessee Online):
    www.vic.com/tnchron/tnstate.htm

Tennessee Valley Railroad and Museum: www.tvrail.com

Trail of Tears: www.trailoftears.org/

Amusement Parks and Attractions

Dollywood: www.dollywood.com

Jack Daniel Distillery: www.jackdaniels.com

Knoxville Zoo: www.knoxville-zoo.org

Memphis Zoo: www.memphiszoo.org/

Nashville Zoo: www.nashvillezoo.org/

Rock City: www.seerockcity.com

Ruby Falls: www.rubyfalls.com

Tennessee Aquarium: www.tnaqua.org

Warner Park Zoo*: zoo.chattanooga.org

*Type address exactly as given.

INDEX